The Essential

B

500 & 650 Twins

A7, A10, A50 & A65: 1946 to 1973

Your marque expert: Peter Henshaw

VELOCE PUBLISHING
THE PUBLISHER OF FINE AUTOMOTIVE BOOKS

Essential Buyer's Guide Series
Alfa GT (Booker)
Alfa Romeo Spider Giulia (Booker & Talbott)
Audi TT (Davies)
Austin Seven (Barker)
Big Healeys (Trummel)
BMW E21 3 Series (1975-1983) (Reverente, Cook)
BMW GS (Henshaw)
BMW X5 (Saunders)
BSA 500 & 650 Twins (Henshaw)
BSA Bantam (Henshaw)
Citroën 2CV (Paxton)
Citroën ID & DS (Heilig)
Cobra Replicas (Ayre)
Corvette C2 Sting Ray 1963-1967 (Falconer)
Ducati Bevel Twins (Falloon)
Ducati Desmodue Twins (Falloon)
Ducati Desmoquattro Twins (Falloon)
Fiat 500 & 600 (Bobbitt)
Ford Capri (Paxton)
Ford Escort Mk1 & Mk2 (Williamson)
Ford Mustang (Cook)
Ford RS Cosworth Sierra & Escort (Williamson)
Harley-Davidson Big Twins (Henshaw)
Hinckley Triumph triples & fours 750, 900, 955, 1000,
1050, 1200 – 1991-2009 (Henshaw)
Honda CBR600 Hurricane (Henshaw)
Honda CBR FireBlade (Henshaw)
Honda SOHC fours 1969-1984 (Henshaw)
Jaguar E-type 3.8 & 4.2-litre (Crespin)
Jaguar E-type V12 5.3-litre (Crespin)
Jaguar XJ 1995-2003 (Crespin)
Jaguar XK8 & XKR (1996-2005) (Thorley)
Jaguar/Daimler XJ6, XJ12 & Sovereign (Crespin)
Jaguar/Daimler XJ40 (Crespin)
Jaguar Mark 1 & 2 (All models including Daimler 2.5-litre
V8) 1955 to 1969 (Thorley)
Jaguar S-type – 1999 to 2007 (Thorley)
Jaguar X-type – 2001 to 2009 (Thorley)
Jaguar XJ-S (Crespin)
Jaugar XJ6, XJ8 & XJR (Thorley)
Jaguar XK 120, 140 & 150 (Thorley)

Kawasaki Z1 & Z900 (Orritt)
Land Rover Series I, II & IIA (Thurman)
Land Rover Series III (Thurman)
Lotus Seven replicas & Caterham 7: 1973-2013 (Hawkins)
Mazda MX-5 Miata (Mk1 1989-97 & Mk2 98-2001) (Crook)
Mercedes-Benz 280SL-560DSL Roadsters (Bass)
Mercedes-Benz 'Pagoda' 230SL, 250SL & 280SL
MGA 1955-1962 (Sear, Crosier)
MGF & MG TF (Hawkins)
MGB & MGB GT (Williams)
MG Midget & A-H Sprite (Horler)
MG TD, TF & TF1500 (Jones)
Mini (Paxton)
Morris Minor & 1000 (Newell)
New Mini (Collins)
Norton Commando (Henshaw)
Peugeot 205 GTI (Blackburn)
Porsche 911 (930) Turbo series (Streather)
Porsche 911 (964) (Streather)
Porsche 911 (993) (Streather)
Porsche 911 (996) (Streather)
Porsche 911 Carrera 3.2 series 1984 to 1989 (Streather)
Porsche 911SC – Coupé, Targa, Cabriolet & RS Model
years 1978-1983 (Streather)
Porsche 924 – All models 1976 to 1988 (Hodgkins)
Porsche 928 (Hemmings)
Porsche 930 Turbo & 911 (930) Turbo (Streather)
Porsche 944(Higgins, Mitchell)
Porsche 986 Boxster series (Streather)
Porsche 987 Boxster and Cayman series (Streather)
Rolls-Royce Silver Shadow & Bentley T-Series (Bobbitt)
Subaru Impreza (Hobbs)
Triumph Bonneville (Henshaw)
Triumph Stag (Mort & Fox)
Triumph TR7 & TR8 (Williams)
Triumph Thunderbird, Trophy & Tiger (Henshaw)
Vespa Scooters – Classic two-stroke models 1960-2008
(Paxton)
Volvo 700/900 Series (Beavis)
VW Beetle (Cservenka & Copping)
VW Bus (Cservenka & Copping)
VW Golf GTI (Cservenka & Copping)

www.veloce.co.uk

For post publication news, updates and amendments relating to this book please visit www.veloce.co.uk/book/V4136

First published in January 2008. Reprinted January 2014 by Veloce Publishing Limited, Veloce House, Parkway Farm Business Park, Middle Farm Way, Poundbury, Dorchester, Dorset, DT1 3AR, England.
Fax 01305 250479/e-mail info@veloce.co.uk/web www.veloce.co.uk or www.velocebooks.com.
ISBN: 978-1-84584-136-2 UPC: 6-36847-04136-6
Readers with ideas for automotive books, or books on other transport or related hobby subjects, are invited to write to the editorial director of Veloce Publishing at the above address.
British Library Cataloguing in Publication Data – A catalogue record for this book is available from the British Library.
Typesetting, design and page make-up all by Veloce Publishing Ltd on Apple Mac. Printed in India by Imprint Digital.

Introduction & thanks
– the purpose of this book

There are lots of books featuring BSA twins, detailing their history, performance, lineage and the minutiae of their specification, but none of them tell you what to look for when buying one secondhand. That's what this book is about – a straightforward, practical guide to buying a used BSA. It won't list all the correct colour combinations for each year, or analyse the bike's design philosophy, or consider its background as part of a troubled industry – there are excellent books listed at the end of this one which do all of that. However, hopefully it *will* help you avoid buying a dud.

For some, BSA's pre-unit or unit construction twin is the definitive British postwar motorcycle. It didn't have the glamour of a Triumph or Norton (though BSA did its best to counter this with a whole raft of twin-carb tearaway variants) but an A7, A10 or A65 was the bike for everyman. BSA twins took dad to work during the week, and the whole family to the seaside at weekends – that's why so many were hitched up to sidecars. Some had practical touches like a qd (quick detach) rear wheel, full chaincase and (on early A7s) a hinging rear mudguard to make wheel changes easier. These weren't bikes as weekend toys, but as day-to-day transport.

Rocket Gold Star is the most sought-after BSA twin.

That's why a BSA twin can be so rewarding to own today. Apart from the usual nostalgia quotient, they can be very reliable and long-lived machines – a well built and cared for A10 should manage up to 60,000 miles before needing major attention. And there are a whole range of modifications – electronic ignition, better lighting and needle-roller main bearings – that make them better suited to the 21st century. Of course, they still need more love and attention than any modern bike,

An early pre-unit BSA like this A7 can make a reliable classic.

but for many that's part of the attraction. And the hotter twin-carb models, while lacking the solid reliability of the cooking bikes, do offer a genuine coffee bar cowboy experience. Whichever BSA twin you buy – enjoy!

Acknowledgements
Thanks go to all those people who helped, and without whom this book would not have happened. Roger Fogg took all the pictures, and spent a lot of time tracking down BSA owners in his native Cornwall. So thanks go to all of them too: Tom Seward, Don Northcott, George Pengelly, Barry Old, Kevin Crowle, Mervyn Pearce, Len and Mary Dingley, Chris Solway, Kevin Pethick, Gary Gillum, Mike Jenkins and Cecil Rowe. Also to owners of the bikes photographed at the 2007 Banbury Run, who weren't around. Gary Hearl at BSA specialists SRM Engineering (www.srm-engineering.com, 01970 621185) was generous with his time and in-depth knowledge. Peter Old had some useful tips, and kindly lent some BSA brochures, while Tom Seward was a mine of information on the Rocket Gold Star. Finally, thanks, too, to Brian Pollitt of the BSA Owners Club and to Nigel Clark at *Old Bike Mart*.

Many BSAs have spent their lives hitched to a sidecar.

Essential Buyer's Guide™ currency
At the time of publication a BG unit of currency "●" equals approximately £1.00/ US$2.00/Euro 1.50. Please adjust to suit current exchange rates.

Contents

Tall and short riders
Compared to modern bikes, BSA twins are relatively small, especially by current 500/650cc standards, though not especially light. Short riders should steer clear of the 1971 bikes, with their sky-scraping 33in seat height.

Running costs
Surprisingly modest. Even ridden fairly hard, BSA twins will return 50-60mpg, and a gently ridden A7 or A10 will manage a good 70mpg. That gives it a smaller carbon footprint than most modern bikes.

Maintenance
Make no mistake, any bike from this era needs more TLC and sympathy than modern machines. You'll need to change the oil every 1000 miles to maximise engine life, and keep an eye open for things coming loose or going out of adjustment. Not a 'ride it and forget it' sort of bike.

Old bikes need looking after, and BSAs are no exception.

Kick-starting
BSA twins were not fitted with electric start. In any case, a well set-up bike will not be hard to start, though it has to be said that kick-starting is more about technique than strength, especially in relation to the later alternator-equipped machines.

Usability
If you need to do lots of motorway (freeway) miles, then a BSA twin is not for you. However, they can be made into very reliable day-to-day bikes, covering lots of miles without trouble.

Parts availability
Excellent, with many parts still being made.

Parts costs
Good. Spares aren't expensive, though beware of suspiciously cheap parts of unknown provenance.

Insurance group
Go for a classic bike limited mileage policy, such as that offered by Carole Nash or Footman James in the UK, and you won't have to pay much.

Investment potential
Depends on the model. BSA twins (Rocket Gold Star aside) have never had the cult status of a Bonneville or Commando, so it's unlikely they'll ever make the same sort of investment potential. Early sportsters like the Road Rocket should hold their value well, as should an A7 Shooting Star and A10 Golden Flash (especially in the Golden Beige colour). Cooking A50/A65s, and 1971-72 oil-in-frame (OIF) bikes are the cheapest at the time of writing, but few OIFs were built, so they have the better investment potential.

Foibles
BSA twins vibrate and leak oil – that's part of motorcycling folklore. However, most riders aren't bothered by the vibes, which only really intrude at high revs, and a well assembled engine in good condition shouldn't leak.

Plus points
Good value for a classic bike, and the softer single-carb machines are useable day-to-day with the right modifications and sympathetic ownership and riding style. Nice, torquey performance from the 650s (the A7 500 is nice too).

Minus points
Like any motorcycle of this era, the BSA twin needs a lot of looking after (though that can be part of the attraction) and it doesn't have the glitz and charisma of a Triumph or Norton.

Alternatives
If you want a British twin, there are loads of alternatives from Triumph, Norton, AJS, Matchless, et al, all with their own characteristics. BSAs are amongst the best value.

2 Cost considerations
– affordable, or a money pit?

Spares availability on BSA twins is generally good, and the prices are reasonable. The prices quoted here are for good quality parts from a specialist – beware cheaper spares of unknown origin. When restoring a bike, it's the labour costs that mount up, rather than spares prices. If you are prepared to service the bike yourself, a BSA should be quite affordable to run, and all apart from the twin carburettor road burners should manage 50-70mpg.

Complete restoration (basket case to concours) – around ●x10,000	Fuel tank (chrome) ●x229(A10)
Air cleaner element ●x22 (A50/65)	Gasket set (complete) ●x24 (A50/65)
Alternator rotor (Lucas RM21) ●x89 (A50/65)	Gearbox mainshaft bearing ●x16 (A50/65)
Brake shoes (7in tls front, exch) ●x32 (A7/10)	Headlamp shell ●x41 (A50/65)
Battery (12v) ●x29 (A50/65)	Ignition coil ●x25 (A50/65)
Camshaft ●x123 (A7/10)	Mudguard (front, chrome) ●x93 (A10)
Carburettor needle jet ●x6(A50/65)	Mudguard (rear) ●x116 (OIF)
Clutch friction plate (each) ●x8 (A50/65)	Oil pump (SRM billet) ●x257 (A7/10)
Clutch cable ●x14 (A7/10)	Rear chain ●x59 (all twins)
Clutch centre drum ●x32 (A50/65)	Pistons (pr) ●x148 (A10)
Cylinder barrel ●x380 (A10)	Primary chain ●x65 (A50/65)
Electronic ignition (Boyer) ●x80 (A50/65)	Silencer ●x98
Fork stanchions ●x38 (A7/10)	Tank badge (pr) ●x45 (A50/65)
	Valve guide ●x13 (A7/10)
	Valve, inlet ●x19 (A7/10)
	Wiring loom ●x74 (OIF)

Don't be put off by damage – most parts are available ...

... though a few parts, like this side panel, are harder to find now.

In an age where most modern bikes need only an oil check and chain tweak between major services, BSA twins demand a lot more looking after. We live in an age when consumer products keep working without much attention, but old bikes aren't like that. However, compared to many classics, the single-carburettor, lower compression BSA twins – whether unit or pre-unit – can make reliable, everyday bikes, especially if the modern day modifications like electronic ignition, SRM oil pump, and needle-roller main bearing are incorporated. These machines were designed as practical working bikes, which is why they have features like a full chaincase, and single-bolt mounting for the fuel tank, enabling it to be whipped off in a trice.

Of course, even a tweaked BSA will still demand a different mindset to running a modern bike. It might be capable of 100mph or more, but sitting on the motorway for hours at outside lane speeds is asking for trouble. The relationship between bike and rider is based on a constant awareness of how the machine is running: has that nut vibrated loose? Is that the beginnings of a leak from the rocker box? Is the battery overcharging?

BSA's twin can be remarkably long-lived, but only if the oil is changed regularly – every 1000 miles is the recommendation – using a straight monograde oil, not a modern multigrade. This is thought to be a better insurance policy than fitting a modern replaceable oil filter. Frequent oil changes using good quality lube should bring a long engine life – up to 60,000 miles before major attention on a well-built engine.

Plunger Gold Flash; nice for touring.

Sportier twins, such as the Rocket Gold Star, are more demanding.

One of the last, a well restored '71 Lightning.

All these little things are part of BSA ownership, and some owners of modern bikes would dismiss them as needless hassle, but plenty of BSA riders would say they are part of what makes owning one (or indeed most old bikes) more satisfying than a new machine. You develop a relationship with it that is quite different to that with a bike that always starts on the button and never goes wrong. And no BSA twin ever will start on the button because none were fitted with electric start, unlike final versions of the Norton Commando and Triumph Bonneville.

How easy a BSA is to live with depends a great deal on which model you choose to buy. With many older British bikes, there were steady improvements over the years in terms of ease of living, but with BSA twins things are less clear cut. The early A7 and A10 pre-units have magneto/dynamo electrics, with dim (by modern standards) 35w headlights, and comparatively feeble drum brakes. The plunger rear suspension offered as an option until 1956 gives less travel than the more modern swingarm rear end, so both handling and comfort suffer.

But they are also solid, reliable machines, built for day-in, day-out use, and given those 1000-mile oil changes and sympathetic (i.e. not flat-out) riding, are very long-lived. They are tractable, easy to ride in traffic, and economical. The 650, in particular, is fast enough to keep up with modern traffic, with pleasantly torquey performance and happy 70mph cruising. Performance variants – the Road Rocket, Super Rocket and Rocket Gold Star – used a higher compression and bigger valves to extract more performance, all of them with 100mph capability, bringing the brake issue into sharper focus! Pre-unit electrics can be upgraded to 12-volt, though it's less easy to improve the brakes, and if riding in heavy modern traffic, that needs to be borne in mind.

Many of the same comments apply to the unit-construction twins, certainly the softer, single-carburettor A50 and A65 Thunderbolt, with the added benefit of alternator electrics (12-volt from 1966), better brakes and improved forks, plus they are cheaper to buy than the equivalent Triumph. The unit-construction twins vibrate more than their predecessors, and are no more oil-tight, but the single-carb versions (especially the 650) are still quite easy to live with. The higher compression, twin-carb bikes – Lightning, Spitfire and others – are a different kettle of fish, overtuned by BSA in an attempt to keep up with the late-1960s opposition, and certainly fast, but with the penalty of worse vibration and shorter engine life. They need more fettling to keep those twin carburettors in tune as well.

The final BSA twins of 1971-72 had a new frame, new brakes, new styling, and one big disadvantage over the earlier bikes. At 33in, the seat height is only really suitable for six-footers, though those produced in the last few months cut that to 31in. Otherwise, the same comments apply, with the single-carburettor Thunderbolt easier to live with than the twin-carb Lightning.

Be clear about the sort of riding you want to do. For sunny Sunday blasts, and if you enjoy riding hard, then a twin-carb road burner, such as the Spitfire or Lightning, is one of the original hairy British twins, and you are sure to enjoy it. But for gentler use, or touring, go for a Thunderbolt or Golden Flash. With a few well chosen modifications, these can make reliable day-to-day bikes, as long as you don't mind sacrificing some unseen originality. They don't cost a fortune to buy, run or maintain, and if you can live with a little vibration (from the unit-construction T'bolt) and are prepared for the oil changes and a little light fettling, the BSA 650s make good, practical classics.

See Chapter 12 for value assessment. This chapter shows, in percentage terms, the value of individual models in good condition. Prices depend more on condition than model, though exceptions are the A50s (cheaper than average) and the 1962-63 Rocket Gold Star (astronomical). Also, a sports A10, such as the Super Rocket, will always fetch more than a cooking A10 in the same condition.

There were many variations on the BSA twin theme over a long production life, and this chapter also looks at the strengths and weaknesses of each model, so that you can decide which is best for you.

The main division is between the pre-unit A7/A10 built up to 1962 ('63 for the limited production Rocket Gold Star), with the engine and gearbox as separate components, and the unit construction A50/A65 from 1962, with engine/gearbox built as an integral unit. We've treated the 1971-72 A65 as a separate model as, although similar mechanically to the 1960s A65, it was otherwise completely different. There's also mention here of the Ariel Huntmaster and Japanese Meguro series – although not BSAs, and assembled in different factories (on the other side of the world, in the case of the Meguro), they are still part of the BSA twin family.

Range availability

1947-50 A7	1962-65 A65 Star
1948-50 A7 Star Twin	1963-65 A65 Rocket
1950-61 A10 Golden Flash	1964-65 A65 Lightning Rocket
1951-61 A7	1964-70 A65 Lightning
1953-54 A10 Super Flash	1964-65 A65 Lightning Clubman
1954-61 A7 Shooting Star	1965-70 A65 Thunderbolt
1955-57 A10 Road Rocket	1964-65 A65 Spitfire Hornet
1958-63 A10 Super Rocket	1966-67 A65 Hornet
1962-63 A10 Rocket Gold Star	1966-68 A65 Spitfire II, III & IV
1954-59 Ariel FH Huntmaster	1968-70 A65 Firebird
1962-65 A50 Star	1971-72 A65 Thunderbolt
1964-65 A50 Cyclone	1971-72 A65 Lightning
1964-65 A50 Cyclone Clubman	1971 A65 Firebird
1964-65 A50 Wasp	1972 A70 Lightning
1965-70 A50 Royal Star	

1946-1963 pre-unit A7/A10

The original – and longest-lived – BSA twin was launched in late 1946 as a rapid postwar response to the success of Triumph's pre-war Speed Twin. It was simpler than the Triumph, with one camshaft rather than two, and didn't have the same get up and go, but was quieter and held together better. With 26bhp, the four-speed A7 had a top speed of around 85mph and could average a good 60mpg. It had magneto/dynamo 6-volt electrics and was joined by the higher compression Star Twin in 1948, the only A7/A10 to feature twin carburettors.

The big news in 1950 was the arrival of the 650cc A10 (brought out early to beat Triumph's own 650 to market), and the nicely named Golden Flash was an instant hit, with an unstressed 35bhp and plenty of torque. It came with BSA's plunger rear suspension, which offered some limited wheel travel, though not enough to improve the handling. The Flash could top 100mph and returned 50-55mpg even when hitched to a sidecar, which many were. It also proved very reliable and, given frequent oil changes, could run to 100,000 miles on the original crankshaft. At the same time, the 500cc A7 was redesigned along A10 lines.

A7 Shooting Star – well worth seeking out.

A new frame arrived in 1954, complete with swingarm, a great improvement on the plunger, with better forks to match, and the gearbox was now bolted to the frame, not to the rear of the crankcase. The first sports A10, the 40bhp Road Rocket, came in 1956, still with a single carburettor but alloy head, higher compression and other changes to give a tested 109mph. All the twins were fitted with full-width brakes that year – the front was a slight improvement (still marginal for the 100mph 650s) but the cable-operated rear was a little spongy.

A10 Gold Flash with plunger rear suspension.

The A10's bottom end was beefed up for 1958, with a one-piece crankshaft, stronger bearings, and thicker cylinder base flange. These were much better able to withstand tuning, the motors identified by a DA10 prefix to the engine number. That laid the basis for the pre-unit BSA's final fling of road burners, starting with the 43bhp Super Rocket the same year. Perhaps in deference

Not all Gold Flashes came in gold.

to that, the front brake became an 8in item, though it wasn't much more powerful. A more substantial (though still only partial) improvement was the redesigned four-spring clutch of 1959.

There were few significant changes for 1960 and '61, as the new unit-construction twins were on the horizon, but the final A10 variant was the most glamorous of all, and remains the most sought after BSA twin to this day. It was the Rocket Gold Star, a marriage of the Super Rocket's engine (with higher compression

Nicely restored Super Rocket with later tls front brake.

and larger exhaust valves) with close-ratio RRT2 gearbox and Gold Star cycle parts. Although in part a cunning means of using up stock (the Gold Star single was also nearing its end) the RGS became a legend, and today fetches very high prices. In the UK, replica Rocket Gold Stars can fetch ⬤x 5000, genuine bikes ⬤x 8-9000 and concours examples ⬤x 12,000 or more. Period extras (from the factory or BSA specialist of the time Eddie Dow) won't harm the price at all.

Strengths/weaknesses: Pre-unit BSA brakes, suspension and electrics are well down on modern, or even 1960s/'70s standards. This is especially worth bearing in mind when considering one of the performance variants, though apart from a lack of ground clearance on the left-hand side, they handle quite well. The electrics at least can be improved, without detracting from originality, and BSA's pre-unit twin is a pleasant, torquey engine, very tractable and with not much vibration if you stay away from high revs. Also, if looked after, very long-lived.

A7: 97%
A10: 110%
Rocket Gold Star: 300-400% (see text)

1962-1970 unit A50/A65

The unit construction 500cc A50 and 650cc A65 were the ubiquitous BSA twins of the 1960s. Nearly 60,000 A65s were built, and they continued two A10 traditions:

on one hand, a torquey single-carb bike, at home solo or hauling a sidecar; on the other, a highly tuned sports machine for the ton-up boys, though now reaching the limits of the basic layout, which resulted in increased vibration, oil leaks and expensive failures. As for the smaller A50, far fewer were made, as the 500cc class lost out in popularity to the bigger 650s and later 750s, and it was something of a cinderella model in the range. The A50s/65s have a poorer reputation than their predecessors, which has kept prices slightly lower, but with the right modifications (and there are plenty of these, readily available) they can be made reliable and pleasant to ride.

Unit construction A50s rarely appear for sale.

Launched in 1962 as the 32bhp A50 and 38bhp A65 Star, the unit BSA twin had plenty of potential for tuning – the 650 had a relatively short-stroke, which

A ragged but complete A65 can be good value.

Unrestored A65, still in characteristic workhorse mode.

would be taken advantage of later. The four-speed gearbox was built in unit with the engine, making for a clean looking design (though the BSA still looked 'dumpy' compared to a Triumph), there were alternator electrics (still 6-volt at this stage) and a triplex chain primary drive. But the unit twins had been developed in a hurry, and problems with the main bearings soon became apparent – these will have long since been solved, but the ultimate answer, as with the A7/A10, is a needle-roller conversion. The brakes still weren't wonderful, especially on the A50, which had smaller 7in items front and rear. On the upside, the new bikes were lighter than the pre-units (though still not featherweights), easy to start and had good performance, with the same frugal fuel consumption as their predecessors.

The first of many performance variants appeared in 1964, the 45bhp Rocket with higher compression, high-lift cams and a top speed of 105mph. It looked sportier too, with gaitered forks, siamesed pipes and skimpier mudguards. It also had 12-volt electrics, thanks to two 6-volt batteries connected in series. The Rocket was well thought of, and was followed in 1965 by the twin carburettor A50 Cyclone and A65 Lightning, the latter with 48bhp and 110mph, though also increased vibration, which was a warning sign. Both bikes were offered in competition Clubman form, with racing seat and bars, rear-sets and close-ratio gearbox – and most of these were exported to the USA. A hotter still twin arrived in 1966, the 54bhp Spitfire – capable of 120mph, but mechanically fragile and cursed with terrible vibration. Slightly more robust was the Firebird, a nominally off-road version of the Lightning, with 2-into-1 high-level pipes.

Better news that year was improved forks, a new 8in front brake, and 6-plate clutch –12-volt electrics were standard across the range from 1965. Other worthwhile improvements came in 1968; a twin-leading shoe front brake and Lucas 6CA contact breaker points, which allowed more accurate ignition timing. Oil tightness was improved in 1969, with an attempt to tackle vibration the following year, but by now the unit twins were seriously outdated.

Strengths/weaknesses: The single-carb A50/A65s are tractable, economical and fast enough to be fun, with the post-1966 improvements adding to the plus side. On the downside are vibration, oil leaks, high speed longevity, and the fragility of the hotter twin-carb bikes in particular.

A50: 78%
A65: 100%

1971-1972 oil in frame A65

Part of an all-new BSA/Triumph range for 1971, though actually using the same outdated vertical twin power units. Frame, brakes and styling were all new, and the engine oil was carried in the frame's backbone tube. The new frame handled well and came with a fine new fork based on that of BSA's motocrosser. Other worthwhile improvements were a higher capacity oil pump, and indicators, while the new conical hub brakes worked well.

Unfortunately, the new range was poorly developed, and the new frame was far too tall. It gave a seat height of 33in, which made the bikes unusable for all but the very long legged. It was also finished in light grey, which showed every spec of road dirt. As before, there was a single-carb Thunderbolt, a twin-carb Lightning, and an off-road style Firebird, this one also with twin carburettors.

Today, the oil-in-frame A65s have a poor reputation, partly through association with the collapse of an entire industry. This has kept prices down, despite the bike's relative rarity, but they really deserve better. The seat height was lowered from April 1972 – production stopped at the end of that year.

Strengths/weaknesses: Handling, braking and electrics brought up to date (by early 1970s standards) but still prone to high-speed vibration and oil leaks. Poor reputation makes them good value, but rarity may push prices up eventually. A65 (OIF) 82.5%

Last gasp – the '71/'72 BSAs aren't as sought-after.

Indicators, new frame, brakes and styling on the OIF BSA.

1972 A70 Lightning

Very rare, a postscript to the BSA twins story in the form of a 751cc version of the A65, with a 9.5:1 compression. Designed with US flat track racing in mind, just 202 were built, and most of

This '71 Lightning cost just $50 in the USA – needs some TLC, though.

Rarest of them all, the A70.

Only 202 A70s were built, and most were exported to the USA.

them were shipped to the States. The A70 had serious vibration problems, but then it was intended as a competition bike. The engine looks identical to that of the A65, but the A70L engine number prefix is the giveaway – if you've found that, you've found a

rare machine indeed. But still, any bike claiming to be an original A70 should come with convincing documentation as evidence. Some folk refer to these bikes as A75s.

A70: 300% (rough estimate as so rarely for sale)

Ariel Huntmaster/Meguro/Kawasaki

The pre-unit A7/A10 design found its way into other factories. Ariel was part of the BSA group, and from 1954 offered the A10 engine in its own frame and cycle parts as the Ariel Huntmaster. The result was a heavy (410lb) machine that performed very like an A10, and was well built. According to one specialist, Huntmasters seem to have been better cared for than A10s – perhaps they attracted a better class of owner! But few Huntmasters were sold and they don't often come up for sale, though despite their rarity they tend to be cheaper than the equivalent BSA.

Rarer still (at least in Europe and the USA) is the Meguro K-1, a Japanese copy of the A7 launched in 1960. By 1966, Meguro was part of Kawasaki, and the 500cc K-1 had become the 624cc W-1, later offering 53bhp, improved electrics and a 112mph top speed. It was briefly exported to the US as the Kawasaki Commander, though fared better back home in Japan. Production lasted (with left-hand gearchange and twin-disc front end) right up to 1976. A fascinating variation on the BSA twin theme, but you'll be lucky to find one outside Japan.

Ariel: 77%

5 Before you view
– be well informed

To avoid a wasted journey, and the disappointment of finding that the bike does not match your expectations, it will help if you're very clear about what questions you want to ask before you pick up the phone. Some of these points might appear basic, but when you're excited about the prospect of buying your dream classic, it's amazing how some of the most obvious things slip the mind ... Also, check the current values of the model you are interested in the classified ads of classic bike magazines.

Where is the bike?
Is it going to be worth travelling to the next county/state, or even across a border? A locally-advertised machine, although it may not sound very interesting, can add to your knowledge for very little effort, so make a visit – it might even be in better condition than you expect.

Dealer or private sale?
Establish early on if the bike is being sold by its owner or by a trader. A private owner should have all the history, so don't be afraid to ask detailed questions. A dealer may have more limited knowledge of the bike's history, but should have some documentation. A dealer may offer a warranty/guarantee (ask for a printed copy).

Cost of collection and delivery
A dealer may well be used to quoting for delivery. A private owner may agree to meet you halfway, but only agree to this after you've seen the bike at the vendor's address to validate the documents. Conversely, you could meet halfway and agree the sale, but insist on meeting at the vendor's address for the handover.

View – when and where
It's always preferable to view at the vendor's home or business premises. In the case of a private sale, the bike's documentation should tally with the vendor's name and address. Arrange to view only in daylight, and avoid a wet day – the vendor may be reluctant to let you take a test ride if it's wet.

Reason for sale
Do make it one of the first questions. Why is the bike being sold and how long has it been with the current owner? How many previous owners?

Condition
Ask for an honest appraisal of the bike's condition. Ask specifically about some of the check items described in Chapter 9.

All original specification
A completely original BSA twin will be worth more than a modified one, but certain mods (SRM oil pump, electronic ignition) can also indicate a conscientious owner who has been actively riding/caring for the machine.

Matching data/legal ownership

Do frame, engine numbers and licence plate match the official registration document? Is the owner's name and address recorded in the official registration documents?

For those countries that require an annual test of roadworthiness, does the bike have a document showing it complies (an MoT certificate in the UK, which can be verified on 0845 600 5977)?

One thing you won't have to worry about in the UK is road tax – everything built before 1973 is, at the time of writing, exempt, which covers all BSA twins.

Does the vendor own the bike outright? Money might be owed to a finance company or bank: the bike could even be stolen. Several organisations will supply the data on ownership, based on the bike's licence plate number, for a fee. Such companies can often also tell you whether the bike has been 'written off' by an insurance company. In the UK these organisations can supply vehicle data:

HPI – 01722 422 422 – www.hpicheck.com
AA – 0870 600 0836 – www.theaa.com
RAC – 0870 533 3660 – www.rac.co.uk
Other countries will have similar organisations.

Unleaded fuel

Has the bike been modified to run on unleaded fuel?

Insurance

Check with your existing insurer before setting out – your current policy might not cover you if you do buy the bike and decide to ride it home.

How you can pay

A cheque/check will take several days to clear and the seller may prefer to sell to a cash buyer. However, a banker's draft (a cheque issued by a bank) is as good as cash, but safer, so contact your own bank and become familiar with the formalities that are necessary to obtain one.

Buying at auction

If the intention is to buy at auction see Chapter 10 for further advice.

Professional vehicle check (mechanical examination)

There are often marque/model specialists who will undertake professional examination of a vehicle on your behalf. Owners clubs may be able to put you in touch with such specialists.

6 Inspection equipment

– these items will really help

This book
Reading glasses (if you need them for close work)
Overalls
Digital camera
Compression tester
A friend, preferably a knowledgeable enthusiast

Before you rush out of the door, gather together a few items that will help as you work your way around the bike. This book is designed to be your guide at every step, so take it along and use the check boxes in Chapter 9 to help you assess each area of the bike you're interested in. Don't be afraid to let the seller see you using it.

Take your reading glasses if you need them to read documents and make close up inspections.

Be prepared to get dirty. Take along a pair of overalls, if you have them. If you have the use of a digital camera, take it along so that later you can study some areas of the bike more closely. Take a picture of any part of the bike that causes you concern, and seek a friend's opinion.

A compression tester is easy to use. It screws into the spark plug holes, and on a BSA twin these couldn't be easier to get to. With the ignition off, turn the engine over on full throttle to get the compression reading.

Ideally, have a friend or knowledgeable enthusiast accompany you: a second opinion is always valuable.

Spotting a fake

However good the condition of the bike, however well it's been restored, there's not much point in going any further if it's pretending to be something it isn't. That's something that BSA twins are liable to – they all used the same basic engine, so it's relatively easy to dress up a cooking A10 or A65 into a Road Rocket, Super Rocket or Lightning.

Be especially wary of a bike described as a Rocket Gold Star, as these are worth two or three times as much as any other model. Look for the rev counter drive off the oil pump (used only by RGS and Super Rocket engines). The frame should not have a kink on its right-hand side – Gold Star singles had this to clear their oil pump, Rocket Gold Stars didn't. The chrome sports mudguards have a beaded edge on the lower edge of the front guard, and the trailing edge of the rear. The petrol tank should be a 4-gallon item in silver with butterfly nut racing snap-filler cap. Finally, the frame number should start with a GA10 prefix and the engine number with D10R (though the latter was shared with the Super Rocket).

On all BSA twins look for the frame number on the left-hand side of the headstock or front engine mounting lug. On 1967-on bikes, this should carry the same number as the engine, and if it doesn't the frame has had a different engine fitted at some point – there may have been a good reason for this, but not having matching engine/ frame numbers reduces a bike's value.

Rev counter drive is an identifier for the Rocket Gold Star and Super Rocket.

However, finding non-matching numbers doesn't necessarily mean it's time to walk away. The bike itself may still be an honest machine with plenty to offer – you just need to make it clear to the seller that you know it isn't 100% original and start negotiating on price.

Documentation

If the seller claims to be the bike's owner, make sure he/she really is by checking the registration document, which in the UK is V5C. The person listed on the V5 isn't necessarily the legal owner, but their details should match those of whoever is selling

'DA10 R' denotes RGS or Super Rocket motor, 'HHC' stands for high compression.

the bike. Also use the V5C to check the engine/frame numbers.

An annual roadworthiness certificate – the 'MoT' in the UK – is handy proof not just that the bike was roadworthy when tested, but a whole sheaf of them gives evidence of the bike's history, when it was actively being used, and what the mileage was. The more of these come with the bike, the better.

General condition

Put the bike on its centre stand, to shed equal light on both sides, and take a good, slow walk around it. If it's claimed to be restored, and has a nice shiny tank and engine cases, look more closely – how far does the 'restored' finish go? Are the nooks and crannies behind the gearbox as spotless as the fuel tank? If not, the bike may have been given a quick smarten up to sell. A generally faded look all over isn't necessarily a bad thing – it suggests a machine that hasn't been restored, and isn't trying to pretend that it has.

Now look at the engine – by far the most expensive and time consuming thing to put right if anything's wrong. A lot of people will have told you that all old British bikes leak oil, but there shouldn't be any serious leaks if the engine is in good condition and has been put together well. Oil misting from the joints is nothing to worry about, but the engine shouldn't be spattered with lube, or have oily drips underneath. Even if it's dry on top, get down on your knees and have a peek at the underside of the crankcase – nice and dry, or covered in oil?

Take the bike off the centre stand and start the engine – it should fire up within two or three kicks, and rev up crisply and cleanly without showing blue or black smoke. Some top end clatter is normal on A65s, but listen for rumbles and knocks from the bottom end, and clonks from the primary drive – any of these are the precursors to serious work. While the engine's running, check that the ignition light or ammeter show that the electrics are charging, and that the oil light (on '69-on bikes) goes out.

Switch the engine off and put the bike back on its centre stand. Check for play in the forks, headstock and swingarm. Are there leaks from the front forks or rear shocks? Are details like the seat, badges and tank colour right for the year of the bike? (A little research helps here, and the reference books listed at the end of this volume have all this information.)

8 Key points
– where to look for problems

Are the screw heads chewed up or the bolt heads rounded-off? Is there damage to the casings around them? All are sure signs of a careless previous owner with more enthusiasm than skill, coupled with a dash of youthful impatience. Not a good sign.

On a post-1966 bike, do the engine and frame numbers match? It's not the end of the world if they don't, but if they didn't leave the factory together it will reduce the value of the bike, however good its condition. On all bikes, do the numbers match those on the documentation?

Listen to the engine running. Clonks or rumbles from the primary drive may indicate wear in the clutch and its shock absorber, the engine sprocket chattering on worn splines, or a loose alternator rotor.

If described as a Rocket Gold Star, is it genuine? As described in Chapter 9, check the frame, the mudguards and engine/frame numbers.

Minor oil leaks aren't a problem (though they are a bargaining point), but serious ones suggest correspondingly serious mechanical wear, or neglect.

9 Serious evaluation
– 30 minutes for years of enjoyment

Circle the Excellent, Good, Average or Poor box of each section as you go along. The totting up procedure is detailed at the end of the chapter. Be realistic in your marking!

Engine/frame numbers

Ex	Gd	Av	Po
4	3	2	1

If there's a golden rule to buying a secondhand BSA – and you want a genuine, original bike – it's to check that the engine and frame numbers match those on the documentation. Unlike Triumphs, the engine and frame didn't use the same numbers until the 1967 model year, but after that date, matching numbers indicate that engine and frame were bolted together on the Small Heath production line, and have stayed together ever since. That's why some classified ads state 'matching engine/frame numbers' – it's a good selling point.

If the numbers don't match, you may still have a perfectly good, functioning motorcycle, and there may be a perfectly good reason for mismatching numbers, such as a replacement engine. But the engine and frame are likely to be from different years, and the engine may not be to the exact specification of the model you're looking at. That's no great disaster if you're not that bothered about complete originality, but it should be reflected in the price, and the bike will be more difficult to sell when the time comes. For pre-'67 bikes, use the table in Chapter 17 to check that engine and frame were built in the same year.

Frame number isn't obvious, but it's there.

Engine and frame numbers are always stamped on, not to be confused with (for example) the raised number on the back of the cylinder barrel. The engine number is located on the left-hand side, just below the cylinder barrel joint; the frame number's also on the left, at the top of the downtube by the steering head on pre-'65 bikes, on the front engine mounting lug for 1965-70, and on the steering head for '71-on. It's sometimes tricky to decipher, especially if the frame has been repainted or powder coated, but it is there.

Engine number should be clear and not tampered with.

Now get down on the ground (it's why you brought the overalls). BSA crankcases come in two halves – right and left – each with a number. On pre-units, the numbers are underneath the dynamo mounting; on units, they are right at the base of the crankcase, on one of the bolt bosses. If these two numbers match, then the two crankcase halves left the

Unit engine numbers are found here.

Unit frame number.

factory together. That's good news, because they were machined as a matching pair, and will fit together nice and snug. If they don't, manufacturing tolerances mean that the cases won't fit well, giving a step on the cylinder barrel flange joint, and a misaligned camshaft tunnel. If the mismatch isn't too bad, the cases can be remachined to suit each other, but there's no guarantee that they can.

It's also worth bearing in mind that the main engine number might be correct, but with a mismatched right-hand crankcase. One more tip – you might find a code number stamped on the tappet cover or outer timing cover. This could be a job number from BSA specialist SRM Engineering – if so, it will be able to confirm what work was done on that bike, and when.

Paint

Some BSA twins look a little 'dumpy', but they can still be handsome machines, especially if the paintwork is in good condition. The good news is that there's not that much of it, just tank, side panels and mudguards. The chrome side panels on many fuel tanks (a BSA hallmark) reduce the area of paint, and many sports twins had chromed rather than painted mudguards as well.

Sometimes a complete respray is the only remedy.

Can you live with minor blemishes?

Having said that, don't underestimate the cost of a professional respray, which is well worth having done, as the fuel tank in particular is such a focal point of the whole bike. So look for evidence of quick and cheap resprays. Light staining around the filler cap, from spilt fuel, might polish out, but could also require a respray. Generally faded original paintwork isn't necessarily a bad thing, and in fact some riders prefer this unrestored look – there are so many restored bikes around, that an honest-looking original, even if a little faded around the edges, has its own appeal.

You may be looking at a bike which has been resprayed in a non-standard colour. If you want 100% originality, then you'll need to research what was the correct colour for the year and model. Use the reference books listed in the back of this volume. Paint availability shouldn't be a problem, as there are often modern equivalents to the original BSA shades.

Chrome

When these bikes were new, chrome was a major styling element, used on the silencers, headlight shell, handlebars, tank side panels, mirrors,

Many BSAs have chrome tank panels.

some mudguards, tank badges and other parts. The quality of the original plating is generally pretty good, though at a minimum of 35 years since new, don't expect it to be pristine.

Whichever bike you're looking at, check the chrome for rust, pitting and general dullness. Minor blemishes can be polished away, but otherwise you're looking at a replating bill. If the silencers are seriously rotted, it's a better idea to budget for a new pair – less hassle than getting the old ones replated in any case.

Tinwork

Ex	Gd	Av	Po
4	3	2	1

There's not a lot of tinwork to worry about on a BSA twin – they were never offered with the 'bathtub' rear enclosure of the equivalent Triumph, for example. However, some A7s and A10s did have a nacelle over the headlamp (not as elegant as Triumph's version) – check this for rust and damage, as finding a replacement could be tricky.

Mudguards too, should be straight, free of rust, and securely bolted to the bike. The early A7's rear mudguard hinged up to ease wheel changes, a typically practical BSA touch. Check that the hinges haven't seized. Full chain enclosure was another practical feature, and an option on pre-units – they are rare now, as many were thrown away by coffee bar cowboys. Unit twins up to 1968 used fibreglass side panels – check that these aren't cracked.

Mid-'60s units used fibreglass side panels.

The oil tank should be checked for leaks through the seams, as repair entails removal and flushing out before it can be put right. From '71 on, the side panels were flat (still in plain black), and covers only, as the oil tank was now part of the frame. Don't expect the two panel halves to line up precisely!

The fuel tank needs to be checked for leaks around the tap and along the seams, as well as dents and rust. Watch out for patches of filler. As with the oil tank, repairing leaks means flushing the tank out (which has to be thorough – you don't want any petrol vapour hanging about when the welding torch is fired up) but the fuel tank is at least easier to remove. Pinhole leaks can often be cured by Petseal, but anything more serious needs a proper repair. If the tank is beyond saving, new ones are available, though not for all models, and this isn't a cheap option once it's been painted either. So a very poor condition tank is a good bargaining lever.

Alloy tank on a cafe racerised Lightning.

Badges/trim

Ex	Gd	Av	Po
4	3	2	1

If the bike you're looking at has missing tank badges, or the side panel transfers are half rubbed off, don't despair. New tank badges are available, though their quality can be variable. A whole variety were fitted over the years, from the original winged BSA motif on the first A7s, through different styles of plastic badge through the 1950s and early '60s, to die-cast aluminium items in 1968 and finally back to the

These rubber plugs are readily available.

Rare transfers may be stocked by the VMCC or BSA Owners Club.

plain winged BSA for the oil-in-frame bikes. Bikes with fibreglass tanks had the BSA star badge as a transfer.

In fact, BSA was very fond of transfers, culminating in such masterpieces as the Super Rocket's Dan Dare style space rocket, blasting off from the top of the fuel tank. In the UK the BSA Owners Club and Vintage Motorcycle Club (VMCC) both run excellent transfer services, which can replace many of these rare adornments.

Seat

Ex	Gd	Av	Po
4	3	2	1

Another key appearance item, something else that varied from year-to-year and model-to-model. Until 1951, all BSA twins used a solo saddle and pillion pad, which was an option right up to 1963. Most bikes have a dualseat, bolted to the frame, and only the 1971-72 bikes have a hinged seat. Most were black, though unit A50s and some A65s had a grey seat. Sports models often had a humped seat, something fitted to all twins from 1967. A grabrail was optional from 1954, but not made standard until much later.

Specialists can re-cover torn seats ...

Whichever seat the bike has, the points to look for are the same. The metal pan can rust, which will eventually give way, though this is easy to check. Covers can tear and split, which of course allows rain in, which the foam padding soaks up ... and never dries out. That's a recipe for a permanently wet backside, or a rock hard seat on frosty mornings (the author speaks from experience). New covers and complete seats in various styles are available. If you can't get hold of a seat in the correct style, corroded pans can

... or supply a new one.

be welded back into shape, and torn covers replaced – both are specialist jobs.

Rubbers

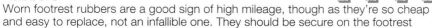

Ex	Gd	Av	Po
4	3	2	1

Worn footrest rubbers are a good sign of high mileage, though as they're so cheap and easy to replace, not an infallible one. They should be secure on the footrest

Worn footrest rubbers indicate high mileage.

Check gearchange rubber is in place.

and free of splits or tears. If the footrest itself is bent upwards, that's a sure sign the bike has been down the road at some point, so look for other telltale signs on that side. The kick-start and gearchange rubbers are also easy to replace, so well worn ones could indicate owner neglect. Beware a worn smooth rubber on the kick-start – your foot's liable to slip off while kicking the bike over, with painful results as the kick-start lever slams back into your leg. The rubber should also be firm on the lever and not drop off after half a dozen kicks. Of course, if the engine needs that many kicks to fire it up, then something's wrong there anyway.

Frame

4 3 2 1

BSA twins used four basic types of frame, all of them conventional duplex (i.e. twin downtubes) tubular steel cradle types, with no serious weaknesses. The early frames differed according to whether plunger suspension was fitted. From 1954, the new swingarm frame was introduced, and the frame for unit bikes from 1962 was broadly similar. There were detail differences between models – the A10 Spitfire, for example, had some fittings trimmed off to lose weight. And of course, the RGS had its very own Gold Star-based frame. From 1971, the oil-bearing frame was completely different, though it too was a tubular steel duplex.

The frame should be checked for rust, cracks and bends.

The most important job is to check whether the main frame is straight and true. Crash damage may have bent it, putting the wheels out of line. One way of checking is by an experienced eye, string and/ or a straight edge, but the surest way to ascertain a frame's straightness is on the test ride – any serious misalignment should be obvious in the way the bike handles. BSAs often had a sidecar hitched up, so even if there's no chair now check the frame downtubes haven't been squeezed by sidecar mounting clamps. Chair use also puts extra stress on the frame, so if the bike has been used in this way, check for cracks and bends.

On all frames, check for bent brackets, which can be heated and bent back into shape, and cracks around them, which can be welded. Those for horn and exhaust pipes are usually the first to succumb to vibration.

Scuffed plunger frame, but in keeping with the rest of the bike.

A frame that is really shabby necessitates a strip down and repaint, though as with the other paintwork, if it's original and fits in with the patina of the bike, then there's a good case for leaving it as it is.

Sidecar

As mentioned above, BSAs were favourites for hauling sidecars, thanks to their rugged build and torquey engines. Some still are, and if you're looking at a complete sidecar outfit, check the chair's frame and mounts for tightness, cracks and bends. If you haven't piloted an outfit before, don't be surprised if it pulls to the right on braking,

A sidecar outfit can add another dimension to motorcycling.

Sidecar mounts must be tight and secure.

and the left on acceleration – they all do that. However, the whole unit should run straight and true at steady speeds, without wandering, and should not be unduly upset by bumps. If you're used to a solo, sidecar outfits take some getting used to, but they do have a certain charm.

Stands

All BSA twins were fitted with both centre and side stands, all of which were conventional, with no particular weaknesses. The exception was the very early A7, whose single-leg centre stand retracted into the seat tube via its spring. It was awkward to use, and if the spring failed could drop down and act as an effective sprag. Fortunately, this arrangement was soon ditched in favour of a conventional pivoting stand.

Both stands should be secure, and when on the centre stand, the bike shouldn't wobble or lean, a sign of serious stand wear and/or imminent collapse. This particularly affects bikes which have been started and left idling on the centre stand – all the vibration is transmitted to ground via the stand, which doesn't do it much good. Pivot holes will probably be worn and the stands themselves may be bent.

Centre stand pivot should be well greased and unwobbly.

Lights

Don't expect modern 100w performance from the original 35w headlight, but it should flick on without hesitation – flickering suggests poor contacts, either in the switch or wiring. Check

that the brake light works – from the rear brake only on pre-'69 bikes, from front and rear thereafter. Two handy modifications will enhance a BSA twin's lighting without altering the outward appearance. A 35w halogen bulb gives a far brighter light than standard, but won't overstress the pre-units' 60w dynamo. Also worthwhile is an LED rear/stop light bulb, a straight swap

Rear light types changed over the years.

for the standard bulb, which takes only minimal power but won't blow, leaving you taillight-less on a dark night.

Check headlight reflector condition.

Electrics/wiring

British twins aren't renowned for dependability when it comes to electrics, and the BSAs were no better nor worse than average. They were gradually updated over the years: the pre-unit twins used magneto ignition and dynamo charging (though a few police models had alternators); units had alternators and coil ignition, and a big step forward was a 12-volt system with zener diode control, standard from 1965. 1968 saw the

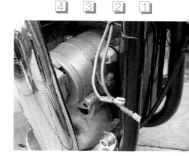

Lucas 6CA contact breakers, which allowed independent adjustment of the spark for each cylinder, and thus more accurate timing – however, the real answer to this is electronic

Wiring connections should be clean and tight.

ignition, which will improve starting, running, smoothness and fuel economy. An electronic system can take up to 2 amps, which could be too much for the original dynamo – one answer is to use a 35w halogen headlight bulb and LED rear light, which should leave enough power left over. Dynamos can also be converted to 12-volt.

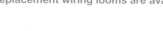

Replacement wiring looms are available.

6-volt magneto on pre-units.

However, the electrical system still needs checking. A good general indication of the owner's attitude is the condition of the wiring – is it tidy and neat, or flopping around? The many bullet connectors need to be clean and tight, and many odd electrical problems are simply down to bad connections or a poor earth. An ammeter was fitted to pre-'71 bikes, though this gives only a vague indication of what's going on. To be sure that the dynamo/alternator is charging as it should, connect a voltmeter across the battery: it should read 12.5-volts with the ignition off, 13-14-volts with the engine running. Battery acid stains on the chain guard or rear mudguard are a sign that the battery has been overcharged.

Finally, check that everything works: lights, horn, indicators (fitted 1971-72, but often removed by owners) and stop light (water can enter the rear brake switch).

Wheels/tyres

Ex [4] Gd [3] Av [2] Po [1]

All BSA twins used spoked wheels with chromed steel rims. Check the chrome condition on the rims – rechroming entails a complete dismantle and rebuild of the wheel. Check that none of the spokes are loose, and give each one a gentle tap with a screwdriver – any that are 'offkey' will need retensioning.

Tyres should be to at least the legal minimum. That's at least 1mm of tread depth across at least three-quarters of the breadth of the tyre. Or if the tread doesn't reach that far across the breadth (true of some modern tyres) then any tread showing must be at least 1mm deep. Beware of bikes that have been left standing (especially on the side stand) for some

A tyre this worn needs replacing.

Check spokes aren't bent or loose.

time, allowing the tyres to crack and deteriorate – it's no reason to reject the bike, but a good lever to reduce the price. If the bike's been standing for years rather than months, the tyres will have gone hard – they may look fine and have plenty of tread, but they won't grip – if you can't stick a fingernail into the rubber, budget for a new set. New tyres in the correct sizes are readily available.

Wheel bearings

Ex [4] Gd [3] Av [2] Po [1]

Wheel bearings aren't expensive, but fitting them is a hassle, and if there's play

Wheel bearing check.

it could affect the handling. To check them, put the bike on its centre stand, put the steering on full lock and try rocking the front wheel in a vertical

Don't forget the rear wheel bearings.

plane, then spin the wheel and listen for signs of roughness. Do the same for the rear wheel.

Steering head bearings

Again, the bearings aren't hugely costly, but trouble here can affect the handling, and changing them is a big job. With the bike on the centre stand, swing the handlebars from lock to lock. They should move freely, with not a hint of roughness or stiff patches – if there is, budget for replacing the bearings. To check for play, put the steering on full lock, grip the front wheel and try rocking it back and forth. Some specialists offer a taper-roller conversion for the steering head bearings, which will make the steering more precise, and will last a long time.

Ex Gd Av Po
4   3   2   1

Play at the steering head bearings may be adjusted out.

Swingarm bearings

Ex Gd Av Po
4   3   2   1

Another essential for good handling are the swingarm

bearings. These are Silentbloc rubber bushes on pre-'69 bikes, which are a hassle to replace as the old ones have to be burnt out. From 1969, the swingarm was fitted with conventional steel-backed bearings – these should have been regularly greased, and if they haven't, rapid wear or even seizure can result, the latter if the bike has been left standing for some time. They are easier to replace,

Play at the swingarm is a major job to put right.

however. To check for wear, get hold of the rear end of the arm on one side and try rocking the complete swingarm from side to side. There should be no perceptible movement.

Suspension

Over a 25-year production run, the BSA twins illustrated the complete evolution of motorcycle rear suspension at the time. The very early pre-units had rigid rear ends – i.e. no suspension at all – but from 1949 plunger rear suspension was an option, and standard from 1952. The plungers offer limited travel, but were a slight improvement on the rigid system. They rarely wear out. Finally, from 1954, a swingarm with twin dampers was optional, and by the late '50s was almost universal.

Check forks move smoothly, without play.   **Rear shock check.**

Front forks had their own evolution, with detail improvements through the 1950s, gaiters appearing in 1964, two-way damping in '66 and shuttle damping in '69. The rear shocks changed little, apart from losing their shrouding in 1969. From '71, to go with the new oil-bearing frame were Ceriani type forks with exposed stanchions. These did a good job, but suffered from exposure to British weather.

Check both forks and rear shocks for leaks. The chrome plate on the fork stanchions eventually pits, especially when exposed to the elements and if the bike has been used in winter. When that happens, it rapidly destroys the oil seals – hence the leaks. New stanchions, or reground and replated existing ones, are the answer, as there's little point in fitting new seals to rough forks.

Check for play by putting the front brake on and trying to rock the forks back and forth; play here indicates worn bushes. Worn out rear shocks will manifest themselves as a weave over 70mph, and sick forks will likewise spoil the bike's handling.

Instruments

Ex Gd Av Po
4 3 2 1

Most BSA twins came with minimal instrumentation – speedometer and ammeter – though a rev counter was optional on the later sporting pre-units, and standard on the twin-carb units. There were various styles, depending on year.

Checking the speedo works obviously has to wait for the test ride – if nothing is working, the cable is the most likely culprit, but if either mileometer or speedo have ceased to function, but the other is still working, then there's something wrong internally – instrument repair is best left to a specialist. Several

Speedometer and ammeter – all you get on the cooking BSA twins.

Ammeters give an indication of electrical health, but they're not infallible.

Leave instrument repair to a specialist.

of these advertise in the classic motorcycle press, and reconditioning a speedo/rev counter set costs £200-£250 in the UK. A battered and bent chrome bezel suggests that a previous owner has had a go themselves.

Engine/gearbox – general impression

Ex Gd Av Po
4 3 2 1

You can tell a lot about the likely condition of a BSA twin without hearing it run. These engines are easy to work on, which encourages owners, whose enthusiasm surpasses their skill, to take things apart themselves, often without the proper tools. So look for chewed up screw or allen bolt heads, and rounded off bolts, plus damage to the casings surrounding them.

It's part of motorcycling folklore that old British twins leak oil, but it doesn't have to be like that. As long as the engine is in good condition and has been properly put together, with matched casings and quality gaskets, it should be reasonably oil tight. The exception is the rev counter drive takeoff, which is difficult to seal. On the engine joints, some light misting isn't a bad sign, but if the bike has a puddle of oil underneath it, and the

Not all old British bikes leak oil.

On the other hand, some do ...

Look for evidence of leaks.

engine/gearbox is covered in lubricant, then walk away; unless, of course, the price reflects the condition. An engine like that is likely to need a complete rebuild. An apparent leak from the gearbox sprocket could actually be excess oil from the camshaft breather. Worn bores or piston rings lead to higher crankcase pressure, pumping oil out through the breather.

Clean and tidy unit engine.

If the engine is described as 'rebuilt', get receipts, and better still, contact whoever did the job to verify that the work was done on this bike. Even buying from a classic bike dealer is no guarantee that a clean-looking engine really has been rebuilt. Some 'restorations' are cosmetic only.

If there's no air filter fitted, that's not a good sign, and without one even a well-built engine will fail prematurely. But with an air filter in place, a well-built BSA twin should give 60,000 miles before needing major attention.

Ask the owner what oil she/he uses, and how often it has been changed. Engines of this era were never designed for modern multigrades – the detergents in these oils will actually pick up dirt from the crankshaft's sludge trap and carry it round the engine. They like straight monogrades, which dump particles in the sludge traps or (an excellent aftermarket addition) the magnetic sump plug. Monograde oils, intended specifically for air-cooled engines of this age, are available from specialists such as Silkolene, Morris or Penrite, so that's what should be used. A monograde oil, changed every 1000 miles, is thought to be a better investment for long engine life than a modern spin-off oil filter. Multigrades also give 15-20psi less oil pressure when hot.

Many of the same comments apply to the gearbox – look for chewed fasteners and signs of neglect. Remove the oil filler cap and stick a finger inside to check whether the oil had been changed recently – nice clean EP90 ... or a frothy sludge? Finally, on pre-units built up to 1956, the gearbox wasn't mounted separately, but bolted to the back of the crankcase via four bolts. The bolt holes can wear, allowing the gearbox to move about. To check this, insert a tyre lever between gearbox and crankcase and waggle it about – any movement should be obvious.

Engine – starting/idling

The engine should start within two or three kicks and settle down to a sweet, rhythmic tickover. If it doesn't, maladjusted contact breaker points, ignition timing or carburettor settings are the most likely culprits – easy to put right, and a knowledgeable owner will already have them spot on. The issue is more complicated on twin carburettor bikes, on which the carbs have to be synchronised to give good starting, clean running and a reliable idle.

Engine should start easily and idle evenly.

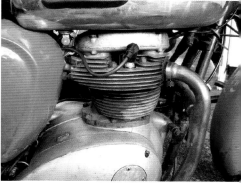

Early unit twin, with smooth (not finned) rocker box.

More seriously, poor starting and idling could be caused by general wear in the carburettor(s), though spares for the Amal carbs used by all BSA twins are easy to find. One alternative (and with little difference in price compared to a reconditioned Amal) is a Mikuni carb conversion – not exactly original, but more efficient than the original, giving more accurate fuelling, easier starting and better consumption.

Poor starting might also be down to low compression, which indicates general wear and will need a top end rebuild to rectify. Take a compression tester along, and use it. Air leaks between carburettor, inlet stubs and air filter are another cause of uneven idling.

Finally, if the bike's been standing a long time (i.e. months) without being run, the sump should be drained first before kicking the engine into life. Over time, oil drains from the oil tank down into the sump which, as it's not compressible, can do nasty things like 'hydraulic' the pistons or blow the crankshaft seal on the primary drive side. At the very least, there will be lots of smoke, and oil will be pumped out of the engine breather all over the garage floor, with very little lube finding its way to the bearings. So, ask the owner when the bike was last started.

Engine – smoke/noise

Air-cooled, pushrod engines of this age produce more mechanical noise than a modern water-cooled motor. However, BSA twins, especially the pre-units with iron cylinder heads, are quieter than most. Expect a little more top end clatter from the alloy-head A7 Shooting Star and sporting A10s, and all unit twins. Another source of A50/A65 noise is from backlash in the timing gears, though this should disappear over idling speed.

Not a BSA, but blue smoke always looks like this.

A sign of real trouble is knocking or rumbling from the bottom end, which will mean a complete engine rebuild for sure. Whether it's big-ends or mains that need attention, the cure is engine out and a complete strip to find out what's wrong. Don't buy a bike that's making these noises unless it's cheap, but engine parts

A leaky engine may still run fine.

Nicely bronzed downpipes – excessive blueness indicates overheating.

to cure all of this – whatever the model – are readily available. The weakest spot on all BSA twins is the timing side crankshaft bush – hence the popularity of needle-roller bearing conversions. If this is worn, oil pressure suffers, but only 1969-on bikes were fitted with a warning light, and there's no way of checking the pressure on the pre-'69s.

Concours pre-unit – but still ride before you buy.

Iron-headed pre-units should be mechanically quiet.

Now look back at the silencers and blip the throttle. Blue smoke means the engine is burning oil and is a sign of general wear in the top end. That means a rebore (again, parts, including oversize pistons, are fully available) but inevitably other problems will come up once the engine is apart – the valves and guides will probably need replacing as well. If you're lucky, the smoke could be down to a badly torqued cylinder head, which will allow oil to be sucked onto the bores from the pushrod tunnel. Black smoke, indicating rich running, is less of a problem, caused by carburettor wear or (fingers crossed) simply a blocked air filter.

Primary drive

Listen to the primary drive while the engine is running. Noises from this area – clonks or rumbles – could indicate a number of problems. It could be wear in the clutch (and its shock absorber on A50/65 unit twins), the engine sprocket chattering on worn splines or (on A50/65s) the alternator rotor coming loose on the crank's driving shaft. Or it could simply be a loose primary chain, either in need of adjustment (via a bolt or screw underneath the chain case on all bikes) or replacement – it's not an expensive item.

Of course, you won't know which of these various troubles is the cause without taking the primary drive cover off, but if the seller acknowledges that a noise is there, it's another good lever to reduce the price.

Listen for clonks and rattles from the primary drive.

Chain/sprockets

With the engine switched off, examine the final drive chain and sprockets. Is the chain clean, well lubed, and properly adjusted? The best way to check how worn it is is to take hold of a link and try to pull it rearwards away from the sprocket. It should only reveal a small portion of the sprocket teeth – any more, and it needs replacing. If the bike is a pre-unit, with the optional full chaincase, check chain tension through the access hole provided.

Check the rear sprocket teeth for wear – if they have a hooked appearance, the sprocket needs replacing. Ditto if any teeth are damaged or missing. If the rear sprocket needs replacing, then the gearbox sprocket will too. Chain and sprockets aren't massively expensive, but changing the gearbox sprocket takes some dismantling time.

Worn chain and sprockets: not serious, but a bargaining point.

Battery

The battery (or in the case of early 12-volt bikes, twin 6-volt batteries) lives under the seat on pre-unit bikes, and behind the left-hand side panel on units. Acid splashes indicate overcharging. The correct electrolyte

Check for acid spills and correct level.

level is a good sign of a meticulous owner, and do check that the battery is securely kept in place by its rubber strap, and that the battery carrier hasn't been corroded by acid over the years.

Ex Gd Av Po
4 3 2 1

Engine/gearbox mountings
These need to be completely solid, with no missing or loose bolts – if they are loose or missing, the bike is not in a rideable condition. The exact design changed over the years but the points to check are the same. All bikes used a cylinder head steady, though the design varied – again, check that it's tight and secure.

Check engine mounts are secure.

Exhaust
Ex Gd Av Po
4 3 2 1

Most BSA twins left the factory with twin silencers, though some, such as the Rocket Gold Star and Lightning Clubman, had a 2-into-1 system. From 1969, all bikes had a balance pipe between the downpipes.

Replacement silencers are no problem ...

Check that the downpipes are secure in the cylinder head (looseness causes air leaks) and examine all joints for looseness and leaks, which are MoT failures. The silencers should be secure, firmly mounted, and in solid condition. Replacements for the various types should all be available.

Test ride
Ex Gd Av Po
4 3 2 1

The test ride should be not less than 15 minutes, and you should be doing the riding – not the seller riding with you on the pillion. It's understandable that some sellers are reluctant to let a complete stranger loose on their

... neither are downpipes, whether individual or siamesed.

pride and joy, but it does go with the territory of selling a bike, and so long as you leave an article of faith (usually the vehicle you arrived in/on) then all should be happy. Take your driving licence in case the seller wants to see it.

Main warning lights
Ex Gd Av Po
4 3 2 1

Modern motorcycles have warning lights for just about everything, but BSA twins don't. Pre-'71 ignition warning lights are there only to tell you that the ignition is on, not whether the battery is charging – the ammeter does that job, though as

Only the '71-72 bikes had a full set of warning lights.

mentioned above, these aren't infallible, giving only a vague indication at moderate revs – check that it shows a positive charge with the lights on. An oil pressure warning light wasn't fitted until 1969 – if there, it should flicker out over idling speed.

Engine performance

A 650cc BSA twin in good condition – whether A10 or A65 – should give good, beefy acceleration in the mid-range. The twin carburettor Lightning and (especially) Spitfire is less tractable at low speed, but all of them should pull cleanly through the mid-range. The 500cc A7 and A50 inevitably have less torque (though the higher compression A7 Shooting Star is a perky performer) but they too should pull cleanly, and easily hold a 60-70mph cruise.

Check for hesitation, which shouldn't happen – a bike with well set up ignition and carburetion will pull crisp and clean. Spitting back through the carbs can be caused by a lack of air filters.

If possible, cruise the bike at 60-70mph for five minutes, then check for oil leaks – there shouldn't be anything more than a slight misting. Expect some vibration at these speeds, but it shouldn't cause numb fingers. Many of the 650s will crack 100mph, but they weren't designed for the motorway age, so it's unfair to expect them to keep up with modern traffic without ill effects for both machine and rider.

All BSA twins should pull cleanly without hesitation.

Clutch operation

As standard, and well adjusted, the BSA clutch won't slip or drag. Slipping is often caused by using ATF (car auto transmission) fluid in the primary drive – use 10/40 or 20/50 oil. Select first gear. A small crunch is normal, but a graunch and a leap forward mean the clutch is dragging. The cure is usually careful

A well tuned BSA twin is a joy to ride.

Lever operation should be smooth, clutch should not drag or slip.

adjustment, though the early six-spring clutch was more inclined to drag. The four-spring clutch fitted from 1960 was better (though it can't be fitted to earlier bikes) as were the three- and four-spring units fitted to A50/A65s. A needle-roller thrust bearing conversion is a worthwhile modification, improving smoothness of take up.

Gearbox operation

Ex 4   Go 3   Av 2   Po 1

There are no particular weaknesses in either pre-unit or unit gearboxes, and given regular oil changes and a well-adjusted clutch, they should deliver a good, positive gearchange. On pre-units, whining is a sign that the bushes are worn, which means regrinding the shafts and fitting undersize bushes. On all gearboxes, watch for false neutrals, or slipping out of gear, a sign of worn gear dogs. If neutral is tricky to find, a slightly dragging clutch won't help – slipping into neutral just before you roll to a stop is often easier than at a standstill.

On the test ride, check that gears engage cleanly and don't jump out.

Handling

Ex 4   Go 3   Av 2   Po 1

BSAs don't have the reputation for sharp handling of their arch rivals Triumph and Norton. But in the case of Triumph, that's not deserved, at least until the mid-1960s when Meriden sorted out the handling of its twins.

Either way, any BSA should steer well, and shouldn't feel soft or wallowy. Faster pre-units had a light front end at very high speeds. Otherwise, any vagueness or weaving will usually be down to worn forks or swingarm bearings, tired rear shocks or the tyres. Rigid and plunger-frame pre-units won't handle mid-corner bumps as well as the swingarm bikes, but that's inevitable. All pre-units, and early units, also suffer from a lack of ground clearance on left-hand bends, thanks to the centre stand.

Brakes

Ex 4   Go 3   Av 2   Po 1

Don't expect modern disc performance from the BSA cable- or rod-operated drum brakes, something which needs to be borne in mind in modern traffic conditions. That said, some of these brakes are better than others.

The pre-unit 7in single-sided drum is reasonably good, though the 7in

'71-72 conical hub brakes work well.

Don't expect modern braking performance from cable-operated drums.

Rear brake should be smooth and progressive.

full-width brake which replaced it isn't as well though of, as it's prone to ovalling (betrayed by a pulsing through the brake lever). Best of all is the twin-leading shoe 8in drum fitted from 1968 (and shared with Triumph), and the oil-in-frame bikes' conical hub in 1971-72, also tls. The '68-on front drum can be fitted to earlier machines.

Ex	Gd	Av	Po
4	3	2	1

Cables

All the control cables – brakes, throttle, choke, advance/retard – should work smoothly without stiffness or jerking. Poorly lubricated, badly adjusted cables are an indication of general neglect, and the same goes for badly routed cables. Note that even new looking cables may not be best quality. If the brake lever comes back to the bars, it's worthwhile replacing the cable as well as relining the brake.

These cables look in good condition, but could do with tidying up.

Switchgear

Ex	Gd	Av	Po
4	3	2	1

Switchgear was very simple on all pre-'71 bikes, limited to a horn/dip switch on the bars, and a lighting and/or ignition switch – the lighting switch later changed from a rotary switch to a toggle in the headlight shell, and the 1971 new generation sported new Lucas alloy switches (confusingly unlabelled at first).

Whatever is fitted, check that it works positively and reliably – early Lucas alloy switches could let water in, with inevitable results. Malfunctioning switches are usually a simple problem to solve, but another reason to bargain over price.

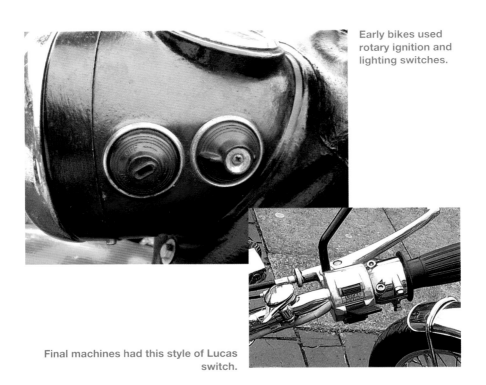

Early bikes used rotary ignition and lighting switches.

Final machines had this style of Lucas switch.

Evaluation procedure
Add up the points scored –

136 = first class, possibly concours; 102 = good/very good; 64 = average; 34 = poor.

Bikes scoring over 95 should be completely useable and require the minimum of repair, although continued maintenance and care will be required. Bikes scoring between 34 and 69 will require a full restoration – the cost of which will be much the same regardless of score. Bikes scoring between 70 and 94 will need very careful assessment of the repair/restoration costs so as to gain a realistic purchase value.

10 Auctions
– sold! Another way to buy your dream

Auction pros & cons

Pros: Prices will usually be lower than those of dealers or private sellers, and you might grab a real bargain on the day. Auctioneers have usually established clear title with the seller. At the venue you can usually examine documentation relating to the bike.

Cons: You have to rely on a sketchy catalogue description of condition and history. The opportunity to inspect is limited and you cannot ride the bike. Auction machines can be a little below par and may require some work. It's easy to overbid. There will usually be a buyer's premium to pay in addition to the auction hammer price.

Which auction?

Auctions by established auctioneers are advertised in the motorcycle magazines and on the auction houses' websites. A catalogue, or a simple printed list of the lots for auctions might only be available a day or two ahead, though often lots are listed and pictured on auctioneers' websites much earlier. Contact the auction company to ask if previous auction selling prices are available as this is useful information (details of past sales are often available on websites).

Catalogue, entry fee and payment details

When you purchase the catalogue of the bikes in the auction, it often acts as a ticket allowing two people to attend the viewing days and the auction. Catalogue details tend to be comparatively brief, but will include information such as 'one owner from new, low mileage, full service history', etc. It will also usually show a guide price to give you some idea of what to expect to pay and will tell you what is charged as a 'buyer's premium'. The catalogue will also contain details of acceptable forms of payment. At the fall of the hammer an immediate deposit is usually required, the balance payable within 24 hours. If the plan is to pay by cash there may be a cash limit. Some auctions will accept payment by debit card. Sometimes credit or charge cards are acceptable, but will often incur an extra charge. A bank draft or bank transfer will have to be arranged in advance with your own bank as well as with the auction house. No bike will be released before all payments are cleared. If delays occur in payment transfers then storage costs can accrue.

Buyer's premium

A buyer's premium will be added to the hammer price: don't forget this in your calculations. It is not usual for there to be a further state tax or local tax on the purchase price and/or on the buyer's premium.

Viewing

In some instances it's possible to view on the day, or days, before, as well as in the hours prior to, the auction. There are auction officials available who are willing to help out if need be. While the officials may start the engine for you, a test ride is out of the question. Crawling under and around the bike as much as you want is permitted. You can also ask to see any documentation available.

Bidding

Before you take part in the auction, decide your maximum bid – and stick to it!

It may take a while for the auctioneer to reach the lot you are interested in, so use that time to observe how other bidders behave. When it's the turn of your bike, attract the auctioneer's attention and make an early bid. The auctioneer will then look to you for a reaction every time another bid is made, usually the bids will be in fixed increments until the bidding slows, when smaller increments will often be accepted before the hammer falls. If you want to withdraw from the bidding, make sure the auctioneer understands your intentions – a vigorous shake of the head when he or she looks to you for the next bid should do the trick!

Assuming that you are the successful bidder, the auctioneer will note your card or paddle number, and from that moment on you will be responsible for the bike.

If it is unsold, either because it failed to reach the reserve or because there was little interest, it may be possible to negotiate with the owner, via the auctioneers, after the sale is over.

Successful bid

There are two more items to think about. How to get the bike home, and insurance. If you can't ride it, your own or a hired trailer is one way, another is to have it shipped using a local company. The auction house will also have details of companies specialising in the transport of bikes.

Insurance for immediate cover can usually be purchased on site, but it may be more cost-effective to make arrangements with your own insurance company in advance, and then call to confirm the full details.

eBay & other online auctions

eBay and other online auctions could land you a BSA at a bargain price, though you'd be foolhardy to bid without examining the bike first; something most vendors encourage. A useful feature of eBay is that the geographical location of the bike is shown, so you can narrow your choices to those within a realistic radius of home. Be prepared to be outbid in the last few moments of the auction. Remember, your bid is binding and it will be very, very difficult to get restitution in the case of a crooked vendor fleecing you – caveat emptor!

Be aware that some bikes offered for sale in online auctions are 'ghost' machines. Don't part with any cash without being sure that the vehicle does actually exist and is as described (usually pre-bidding inspection is possible).

Auctioneers

Bonhams	www.bonhams.com
British Car Auctions (BCA)	www.bca-europe.com or www.british-car-auctions.co.uk
Cheffins	www.cheffins.co.uk
eBay	www.ebay.com (www.ebay.co.uk)
H&H	www.classic-auctions.co.uk
Palmer Snell	www.palmersnell.co.uk
Shannons	www.shannons.com.au
Silver	www.silverauctions.com

11 Paperwork

– correct documentation is essential!

The paper trail

Classic bikes sometimes come with a large portfolio of paperwork which has been accumulated and passed on by a succession of proud owners. This documentation represents the real history of the machine, from which you can deduce how well it's been cared for, how much it's been used, which specialists have worked on it, and the dates of major repairs and restorations. All of this information will be priceless to you as the new owner, so be very wary of bikes with little paperwork to support their claimed history.

Registration documents

All countries/states have some form of registration for private vehicles, whether it's like the American 'pink slip' system or the British 'log book' system.

It is essential to check that the registration document is genuine, that it relates to the bike in question, and that all the details are correctly recorded, including frame and engine numbers (if these are shown). If you are buying from the previous owner, his or her name and address will be recorded in the document: this will not be the case if you are buying from a dealer.

In the UK the current (Euro-aligned) registration document is the V5C, and is printed in coloured sections of blue, green and pink. The blue section relates to the motorcycle specification, the green section has details of the registered keeper (who is not necessarily the legal owner), and the pink section is sent to the DVLA in the UK when the bike is sold. A small section in yellow deals with selling within the motor trade.

In the UK the DVLA will provide details of earlier keepers of the bike upon payment of a small fee, and much can be learned in this way.

If the bike has a foreign registration there may be expensive and time-consuming formalities to complete: do you really want the hassle? More recently, many of the thousands of BSA twins exported to the USA have been advertised for sale here. It sounds like a great chance to buy a bike that has only been used on dry, West Coast roads, with the added glamour of US heritage. However, you'll have to buy the bike sight unseen, and the paperwork involved in importing and re-registering is a daunting prospect. It means employing a shipping agent; you'll also have to budget-in the shipping costs. Then there's (at the time of writing) 6 per cent import duty on the bike and shipping costs, and 17.5 per cent VAT on the whole lot. Unless you're after a rare US-only spec bike, it may not be worth it.

Roadworthiness certificate

Most country/state administrations require that bikes are regularly tested to prove that they are safe to use on the public highway. In the UK that test (the MoT) is carried out at approved testing stations, for a fee. In the USA the requirement varies, but most states insist on an emissions test every two years as a minimum, while the police are charged with pulling over unsafe-looking vehicles.

In the UK the test is required on an annual basis once a vehicle becomes three years old. Of particular relevance for older bikes is that the certificate issued includes the mileage reading recorded at the test date and, therefore, becomes an independent record of that machine's history. Ask the seller if previous certificates are available. Without an MoT the vehicle should be trailered to its new home, unless you insist that a valid MoT is part of the deal. (Not such a bad idea this, as at least you will know the bike was roadworthy on the day it was tested and you don't need to wait for the old certificate to expire before having the test done.)

Road licence

The administration of every country/state charges some kind of tax for the use of its road system, the actual form of the 'road licence' and how it is displayed varying enormously country to country and state to state. Whatever the form of the road licence, it must relate to the vehicle carrying it and must be present and valid if the bike is to be ridden on the public highway legally. The value of the licence will depend on the length of time it will continue to be valid.

In the UK, bikes built before the end of 1972 (which covers all BSA twins) are exempt from road tax, but they must still display a valid disc.

Certificates of authenticity

For many makes of classic bike it is possible to get a certificate proving the age and authenticity (e.g. engine and frame numbers, paint colour and trim) of a particular machine. These are sometimes called 'Heritage Certificates', and if the bike comes with one of these it is a definite bonus. If you want to obtain one, the owners club is the best starting point.

Valuation certificate

Hopefully, the vendor will have a recent valuation certificate, or letter signed by a recognised expert stating how much he, or she, believes the particular bike to be worth (such documents, together with photos, are usually needed to get 'agreed value' insurance). Generally such documents should act only as confirmation of your own assessment of the bike rather than a guarantee of value as the expert has probably not seen it in the flesh. The easiest way to find out how to obtain a formal valuation is to contact the owners club.

Service history

Often these bikes will have been serviced at home by enthusiastic (and hopefully capable) owners for a good number of years. Nevertheless, try to obtain as much service history and other paperwork pertaining to the bike as you can. Naturally, specialist garage receipts score most points in the value stakes. SRM Engineering, for example, can, if given a job number, tell you exactly what work was carried out on a particular bike, and when.

Anything helps in the great authenticity game. Items like the original bill of sale, handbook, parts invoices and repair bills all adding to the story and the character of the machine. Even a brochure correct to the year of the bike's manufacture is a useful document, and is something that you could well have to search hard to locate in future years. If the seller claims that the bike has been restored, then expect receipts and other evidence from a specialist restorer.

If the seller claims to have carried out regular servicing, ask what work was completed, when, and seek some evidence of it being carried out. Your assessment of the bike's overall condition should tell you whether the seller's claims are genuine.

Restoration photographs

If the seller tells you that the bike has been restored, then expect to be shown a series of photographs taken while the restoration was under way. Pictures taken at various stages, and from various angles, should help you gauge the thoroughness of the work. If you buy the bike, ask if you can have all the photographs, as they form an important part of its history. It's surprising how many sellers are happy to part with their bike and accept your cash, but want to hang on to their photographs! In the latter event, you may be able to persuade the vendor to get a set of copies made.

12 What's it worth to you?
– let your head rule your heart!

Condition
If the bike you've been looking at is really tatty, then you've probably not bothered to use the marking system in Chapter 9. You may not have even got as far as using that chapter at all!

If you did use the marking system, you'll know whether the bike is in Excellent (maybe Concours), Good, Average or Poor condition, or, perhaps, somewhere in between these categories.

To keep up to date with prices, buy the latest editions of the classic bike magazines and check the classified and dealer ads – these are particularly useful as they enable you to compare private and dealer prices. Most of the magazines run auction reports as well, which publish the actual selling prices, as do the auction house websites.

Values have been fairly stable for some time, but some models will always be more sought after than others. For example, it's clear that Rocket Gold Stars command the highest prices of all, but if you want an all-round practical classic, then that's not the bike for you. Prices can go down as well as up, but the RGS will probably remain the most sought-after BSA twin of all.

Bear in mind that a bike that is truly a recent show winner could be worth more than the highest price usually seen. Assuming that the bike you have in mind is not in show/concours condition, then relate the level of condition that you judge it to be in with the appropriate price in the adverts. How does the figure compare with the asking price? Before you start haggling with the seller, consider what affect any variation from standard specification might have on the bike's value. This is a personal thing: for some, absolute originality is non-negotiable, while others see non-standard parts as an opportunity to pick up a bargain. Do your research in the reference books, so that you know the bike's spec when it left the factory. That way, you shouldn't end up paying a top-dollar original price for a non-original bike.

If you are buying from a dealer, remember there will be a dealer's premium on the price.

Striking a deal
Negotiate on the basis of your condition assessment, mileage, and fault rectification cost. Also take into account the bike's specification. Be realistic about the value, but don't be completely intractable: a small compromise on the part of the vendor or buyer will often facilitate a deal at little real cost.

13 Do you really want to restore?
– it'll take longer and cost more than you think

There's a romance about restoration projects, about bringing a sick bike back into blooming health, and it's tempting to buy something that 'just needs a few small jobs' to bring it up to scratch. But there are two things to think about: one, once you've got the bike home and start taking it apart, those few small jobs could turn into big ones; two, restoration takes time, which is a precious thing in itself. Be honest with yourself – will you get as much pleasure from working on the bike as you will from riding it?

Of course, you could hand the whole lot over to a professional, and the biggest cost involved there is not the new parts, but the sheer labour involved. Such restorations don't come cheap, and, if taking this route, there are three other issues to bear in mind as well.

First, make it absolutely clear what you want doing. Do you want the bike to be 100 per cent original at the end of the process, or simply useable? Do you want a concours finish, or are you prepared to put up with a few blemishes on the original parts?

Secondly, make sure that not only is a detailed estimate involved, but that it is more-or-less binding. There are too many stories of a person quoted one figure only to be presented with an invoice for a far larger one!

Oh dear. Restorations can start with a box of bent bits.

Third, check that the company you're dealing with has a good reputation – the owners club, or one of the reputable parts suppliers, should be able to make a few recommendations.

Restoring a BSA twin yourself requires a number of skills, which is fine if you already have them, but if you haven't it's good not to make your

Better to start with something more complete than this ...

Minor faults can be corrected between riding sessions.

newly acquired bike part of the learning curve! Can you weld? Are you confident about building up an engine? Do you have a warm, well-lit garage with a solid workbench and good selection of tools?

Be prepared for a top-notch professional to put you on a lengthy waiting list or, if tackling a restoration yourself, expect things to go wrong and set aside extra time to complete the task. Restorations can stretch into years when things like life intrude, so it's good to have some sort of target date.

A rolling restoration makes sense in many ways, especially as the summers start to pass with your bike still off the road. This is not the way to achieve a concours finish, which can only really be achieved via a thorough nut-and-bolt rebuild, without the bike getting wet, gritty and salty in the meantime. But there's a lot to be said for a rolling restoration. Riding it helps keep your interest up as the bike's condition improves, and it's also more affordable than trying to do everything in one go. In the long run, it will take longer, but you'll get some on-road fun out of the bike in the meantime.

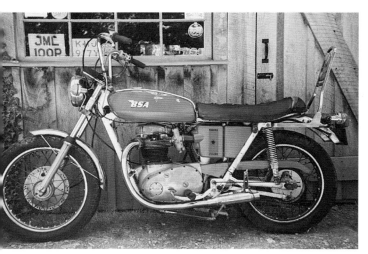

Tatty, but complete and restorable – a potential rolling restoration.

Paint faults generally occur due to lack of protection/maintenance, or to poor preparation prior to a respray or touch-up. Some of the following conditions may be present in the bike you're looking at.

Orange peel

This appears as an uneven paint surface, similar to the appearance of the skin of an orange. The fault is caused by the failure of atomised paint droplets to flow into each other when they hit the surface. It's sometimes possible to rub out the effect with proprietary paint cutting/rubbing compound or very fine grades of abrasive paper. A respray may be necessary in severe cases. Consult a paint shop for advice.

It's not just the tank that may need repainting.

Cracking

Severe cases are likely to have been caused by too heavy an application of paint (or filler beneath the paint). Also, insufficient stirring of the paint before application can lead to the components being improperly mixed, and cracking can result. Incompatibility with the paint already on the panel can have a similar effect. To rectify it is necessary to rub down to a smooth, sound finish before respraying the problem area.

Crazing

Sometimes the paint takes on a crazed rather than a cracked appearance when the problems mentioned under 'cracking' are present. This problem can also be caused by a reaction between the underlying surface and the paint. Paint removal and respraying the problem area is usually the only solution.

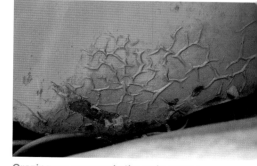

Crazing – a respray is the only answer.

Blistering

Almost always caused by corrosion of the metal beneath the paint. Usually perforation will be found in the metal, and the damage will usually be worse than that suggested by the area of blistering. The metal will have to be repaired before repainting.

Micro blistering

Usually the result of an economy respray where inadequate heating has allowed moisture to settle on the vehicle before spraying. Consult a paint specialist, but damaged paint will have to be removed before partial or full respraying. Can also be caused by bike covers that don't 'breathe'.

Fading

Some colours, especially reds, are prone to fading if subject to strong sunlight for long periods without the benefit of polish protection. Sometimes, proprietary paint restorers and/or paint cutting/rubbing compounds will retrieve the situation. Often a respray is the only real solution.

Peeling

Often a problem with metallic paintwork when the sealing lacquer becomes damaged and begins to peel off. Poorly applied paint may also peel. The remedy is to strip and start again.

Generally faded and tatty paintwork might be worth keeping ...

... but this is a bit too far gone.

Dimples

Dimples in the paintwork are caused by the residue of polish (particularly silicone types) not being removed properly before respraying. Paint removal and repainting is the only solution.

15 Problems due to lack of use
– just like their owners, BSA twins need exercise!

Rust
If the bike is put away wet, and/or stored a cold, damp garage, the paint, metal and brightwork will suffer. Ensure the machine is completely dry and clean before going into storage, and if you can afford it, invest in a dehumidifier to keep the garage atmosphere dry.

Damp storage accelerates rust.

Seized components
Cables are vulnerable to seizure too. The solution is to thoroughly lube them beforehand, and give them a couple of pulls once a week or so.

Operate levers and controls once a week.

Tyres
If the bike's been left on its side stand, most of its weight is on the tyres, which will develop flat spots and cracks over time. Always leave the bike on its centre stand, which takes weight off the tyres. If the tyres haven't been used for years, they eventually go hard, and won't grip – the only solution is new tyres.

Might look good but tyres can lose all grip after long-term storage.

Engine

Old, acidic oil can corrode bearings. Many riders change the oil in the spring, when they're putting the bike back on the road, but really it should be changed just before the bike is laid up, so that the bearings are sitting in fresh oil. The same goes for the gearbox. While you're giving the cables their weekly exercise, turn the engine over slowly on the kickstart, ignition off. Don't start the engine though – running it for a short time does more harm than good, as it produces a lot of moisture internally, which the engine doesn't get hot enough to burn off. This moisture will attack the engine internals, and the silencers.

If the bike's been standing without being started for months, then it may have wet sumped (oil tank content drained into sump), so be sure to drain the sump (not the oil tank) before starting – see Chapter 8.

Battery/electrics

Either remove the battery and give it a top-up charge every couple of weeks, or connect it up to a battery top-up device such as the Optimate, which will keep it permanently fully charged. Damp conditions will allow fuses and earth connections to corrode, storing up electrical troubles for the spring. Eventually, wiring insulation will harden and fail.

16 The Community
– key people, organisations and companies in the BSA world

Auctioneers
See Chapter 10.

Clubs across the world
BSA Owners Club (UK)
www.bsaoc.demon.co.uk
www.bsaoc.org

Australia – New South Wales
www.bsansw.org.au

Australia – South Australia
www.geocities.com/neds1au

Belgium
www.bsaoc.be

Canada
www.geocities.com/MotorCity/Pit/8053

France
Thierry Berthelot, Varaaize 17400, Saint
Jean D'Angely, France

Germany
www.bsa-oc.de

Italy
Mario Di Giovanni, Via Cologno Mon
Sese 174, 00135 Roma, Italy

Luxembourg
Gilbert Bredims, 23 Dreikantonstross, L
8352, Dahlem, Luxembourg

Netherlands
www.bsa-oc.com

New Zealand
Robert Cochrane, PO Box 33-018,
Petone, Wellington, New Zealand

Norway
www.bsaoc.no

Portugal
Paulo Mendes, Apartado 6060,
P-9001-501 Funchal, Portugal

Switzerland
Email: hrvr@kfn-ag.ch

USA
www.bsaoc.org/north_america

Denmark
www.bsa.dk

Czech Republic
www.bsa.webpark.cz

Specialists
There are so many BSA specialists out
there that it would be impossible to list
them all, and we have restricted our
listing to UK companies. Many others
(including some here) are not BSA
specialists but still stock a good line of
BSA spares. This list does not imply
recommendation and is not deemed
to be comprehensive. Most of the
companies listed offer a worldwide mail
order service.

A Gagg & Sons
Spares – Nottingham
www.gagg-and-sons.freeserve.co.uk
0115 9786288

Autocycle Engineering
Spares – West Midlands
01384 253030

Barleycorn
Stainless steel parts – Norfolk
www.barleycorn.co.uk
01379 586728

Bob Price Classic Bikes
A65 spares/restorations – Staffordshire
01538 385939

Britbits
Spares – Bournemouth
www.britbits.co.uk
01202 483675

Burlen Fuel Sytems
Amal carburettor spares
www.burlen.co.uk
01722 412500

C&D Autos
Spares – Birmingham
0121 706 2902
Email: canddautos@eidosnet.co.uk

Draganfly Motorcycles
Spares – Norfolk
www.draganfly.co.uk
01986 894798

Kidderminster Motorcycles
Spares – Herefordshire
01562 66679

Kirby Rowbotham
Electronic ignition/oil filters –
Staffordshire
www.kirbyrowbotham.com
01889 584758

Lightning Spares

Spares – Cheshire
0161 969 3850

SRM Engineering
Spares/engineering/restorations
– Aberystwyth
www.srm-engineering.com
01970 627771

Supreme Motorcycles
Spares – Leicestershire
www.suprememotorcycles.co.uk
01455 841133

Books

BSA Competition History
Norman Vanhouse, Haynes Publishing,
1986

BSA Twin Restoration
Roy Bacon, Osprey Publishing, 1986

BSA Twins & Triples
Roy Bacon, Osprey Publishing, 1980

*British Motorcycles Since 1950, Vols 1
& 2*
Steve Wilson, Patrick Stephens Limited,
1991

*The Illustrated History of BSA
Motorcycles*
Roy Bacon, Promotional Reprint
Company, 1995

17 Vital statistics
– essential data at your fingertips

Listing the vital statistics of every BSA twin variant would take far more room than we have here, so we've picked three representative models: 1957 A7 Shooting Star, 1962 A65 Star, and 1970 A65 Lightning.

Max speed
A7 SS: 94mph
A65 Star: 106mph
A65 Lightning: 101mph

Engine
A7 SS: Air-cooled vertical twin – 497cc, bore and stroke 66 x 72.6 mm, compression ratio 7.25:1, power 32bhp
A65 Star: Air-cooled vertical twin – 654cc, bore x stroke 74 x 75mm, compression ratio 8.3:1, power 38bhp @ 5800rpm
A65 Lightning: Air-cooled vertical twin, 654cc, bore x stroke 74 x 75mm, compression ratio 9.0:1, power 52bhp @ 7500rpm

Gearbox
A7 SS: Four-speed. Ratios: 1st.13.62:1, 2nd 9.28:1, 3rd 6.38:1, 4th 5.28:1
A65 Star: Four-speed. Ratios: 1st 11.1:1, 2nd 7.18:1, 5.13:1, 4.35:1
A65 Lightning: Four-speed. Ratios 1st 12.23:1, 2nd 7.80:1, 3rd 5.58:1, 4th 4.87:1

Brakes
A7 SS: Drums, front 7 x 1.5in, rear 7 x 1.5in
A65 Star: Drums, front 8in, rear 7in
A65 Lightning: Drums, front 8 x 1.62in, rear 7 x 1.12in

Electrics
A7 SS: 6-volt, magneto, 60-watt dynamo
A65 Star: 6-volt, coil ignition, alternator
A65 Lightning: 12-volt, coil ignition, alternator

Weight
A7SS: 448lb
A65 Star: 408lb
A65 Lightning: 443lb

Model introductions and major changes by model year
1947: A7 introduced
1948: A7 Star Twin
1950: A10 Golden Flash
1951: Redesigned A7, based on A10
1952: New engine breather, improved fork damping, black (not chrome) fuel tank late '51-Sept '52

1953: A10 Super Flash. Headlamp semi-nacelle, 8in front brake on A10.
1954: A7 Shooting Star. Swingarm frame, improved forks, single-bolt fuel tank fixing (export only)
1955: A10 Road Rocket. Swingarm frame, improved forks, single-bolt fuel tank fixing (home)
1956: Full-width alloy hubs, 7 x 1.5in brakes, optional chaincase
1958: A10 Super Rocket. Triumph-type full-width cast-iron hubs, 8in front brake (except standard A7), full headlamp nacelle, stronger bottom end with one-piece crankshaft
1960: 4-spring clutch, valanced front mudguard, pear-shaped tank badges (except A7SS)
1962: A10 Rocket Gold Star, A50 Star, A65 Star. Redesigned brakes, 9:1 cr (both changes, A10SR only)
1963: A65 Rocket. Optional 12-volt electrics
1964: A50 Cyclone/Cyclone Clubman, A65 Lightning Rocket (USA), A65 Lightning , A65 Lightning Clubman, A65 Spitfire Hornet
1965: A50 Wasp, A50 Royal Star, A65 Thunderbolt. Two-bolt fixing side panels, 12-volt electrics standard
1966: A65 Spitfire. 3-spring clutch, two-damped forks, improved primary chain adjuster, Lightning-style frame fitted to all twins, humped dualseat
1967: Single 12-volt battery replaces two 6-volt, finned zener diode beneath steering head, 150mph speedometer, finned rocker cover
1968: A65 Firebird. Export styling (smaller fuel tank, high-rise bars, no front licence plate), Lucas 6CA contact breakers, toggle light switch in headlamp, alloy tank badges, Amal Concentric carbs, 8in tls front brake (A65 L and SS)
1969: Unified threads (partial change), thicker crankcase/primary chaincase joints, oil pressure light, tls front brake on all twins, modified forks, swingarm bearings phospor-bronze bushes, steel sidepanels, balance pipe linking downpipes
1970: Thicker cylinder base joint, machined crank and flywheel assembly
1971: New frame and cycle parts (see text)
1972: A75. Black frame (also lowers seat height by 2in), 4-gallon fuel tank

Engine/frame numbers

® – rigid rear end
(pl) – plunger rear end
(sa) – swingarm rear end
(alt) – alternator

(rod) – rod-operated rear brake
(rpm) – with rev counter
C – close-ratio gearbox

Year	Model	Engine	Frame
1947	A7	XA7-101	XA7-101
1948	A7	YA7-101	YA7-101
1949	A7 (r)	ZA7R-101	ZA7-101
	A7 (pl)	ZA7-101	ZA7S-101
	A7ST	ZA7S-101	ZA7S-101
1950	A7 ®	ZA7-7001	ZA7-4001

Year	Model	Engine	Frame
	A7 (pl)	ZA7-7001	ZA7S-6001
	A7ST	ZA7S-4001	ZA7S-6001
	A10 ®	ZA10-4001	ZA7-6001
	A10 (pl)	ZA10-101	ZA7S-101
1951	A7 ®	AA7-101	ZA7-6001
	A7 (pl)	AA7-101	ZA7S-14001
	A7ST	AA7S-101	ZA7S-14001
	A10 ®	ZA10-12001	ZA7S-6001

Year	Model	Engine	Frame
	A10 (pl)	ZA10-4001	ZA7S-14001
1952	A7®	AA7-5001	ZA7-8001
	A7(pl)	AA7-5001	ZA7S-26001
	A7ST	AA7S-1001	ZA7S-26001
	A10®	ZA10-12001	ZA7-8001
	A10(pl)	ZA10-12001	ZA7S-26001
1953	A7®	BA7-101	BA7-101
	A7(pl)	BA7-101	BA7S-101
	A7ST	BA7S-101	BA7S-101
	A10®	BA10-101	BA7-101
	A10(pl)	BA10-101	BA7S-101
	A10SF	BA10S-101	BA10S-101
1954	A7(pl))	BA7-2001	BA7S-8950
	A7(sa)	CA7-101	CA7-101
	A7ST	BA7S-101	BA7S-101
	A7SS	CA7SS-2001	CA7-101
	A10(pl)	BA10-7001	BA7S-8950
	A10(sa)	CA10-101	CA7-101
	A10SF	BA10S-701	BA10S-701
	A10RR	CA10R-101	CA7-101
1955	A7	CA7-1501	CA7-7001
	A7SS	CA7SS-501	CA7-7001
	A10(sa)	CA10-4501	CA7-7001
	A10(pl)	BA10-11001	BA7S-15001
	A10RR	CA10R-601	CA7-7001
1956	A7	CA7-2701	EA7-101
	A7SS	CA7SS-2301	EA7-101
	A10(sa)	CA10-8001	EA7-101
	A10(pl)	BA10-14001	BA7S-18001
	A10RR	CA10R-2001	EA7-101
1957	A7	CA7-4269	EA7-7392
	A7SS	CA7SS-3500	EA7-7401
	A10(sa)	CA10-11392	EA7-7378
	Last		
	A10(pl)	BA10-16036	BA7S-20289
	A10RR	CA10R-3711	CA7-7327
1958	A7	CA7-5001	FA7-101
	A7SS	CA7SS-4501	FA7-101
	A10	DA10-651	FA7-101
	A10SR	CA10R-6001	FA7-101

Year	Model	Engine	Frame
1959	A7	CA7-5867	FA7-8522
	A7SS	CA7SS-5425	FA7-8522
	A10	DA10-4616	FA7-8522
	A10SR	CA10R-8193	FA7-8522
	A10		
	Spitfire	CA10SR-776	FA7A-101
1960	A7	CA7-7101	GA7-101
	A7SS	CA7SS-6701	GA7-101
	A10	DA10-7801	GA7-101
	A10SR	DA10R-101	GA7-101
	A10		
	Spitfire	DA10SR-101	GA7A-101
1961	A7	CA7-8501	GA7-11101
	A7(alt)	CA7A-8501	GA7-11101
	A7SS	CA7SS-8001	GA7-11101
	A10	DA10-13201	GA7-11101
	A10SR	DA10R-3001	GA7-11101
	A10		
	Spitfire	DA10SR-401	GA7A-401
1962	A7	CA7-9714	GA7-21120
	A7(alt)	CA7A-9714	GA7-21120
	A7SS	CA7SS-9277	GA7-21120
	A10	DA10-17181	GA7-21120
	A10SR	DA10R-5958	GA7-21120
	A10		
	Spitfire	DA10R-5958	GA7A-536
	A10RGS	DA10R5958	GA10-101
	A50	A50-101	A50-101
	A65	A65-101	A65-101
	A50(rod)	A50-101	A50A-101
	A65(rod)	A65-101	A50A-101
1963	A10	DA10-17727	GA7-23643
	A10(alt)	DA10A-17727	GA7-23643
	A10SR	DA10R-8197	GA7-23643
	A10		
	Spitfire	DA10R-8197	GA7A-748
	A10RGS	DA10R-8197	GA10-390
	Last		
	A10RGS	DA10R-10388	GA10-1914
	A50	A50-283	A50-2288
	A65	A65-1947	A65-2288
	A50(rod)	A50-823	A50A-2701
	A65(rod)	A65-1947	A50A-101

Year	Model	Engine	Frame
1964	A50	A50A101	A50-5501
	A50 (police)	A50AP101	A50-5501
	A65	A65A-101	A50-5501
	A65 (police)	A65AP-101	A50-5501
	A65R	A65B-101	A50-5501
	A65R (rpm)	A65C-101	A50-5501
	A65T/R	A65B-101	A50-5501
	A50C (USA)	A50B-101	A50B-101
	A65L/R	A65D-101	A50B-101
	A65SH	A65E-101	A50B-101
1965	A50	A50A686	A50-8437
	A50 (police)	A50AP121	A50-8437
	A65	A65A-1134	A50-8437
	A65 (police)	A65AP-267	A50-8437
	A65R	A65B-334	A50-8437
	A65R (rpm)	A65C-1082	A50-8437
	A50C (USA)	A50D-101	A50B-4001
	A50CC (USA)	A50B-507	A50B-4001
	A50C (UK)	A50DC-101	A50B-4001
	A50CC (UK)	A50DC-101	A50B-4001
	A65L/R	A65D-1742	A50B-4001
	A65SH	A65E-701	A50B-4001
	A65L	A65DC-2158	A50B-4001
	A65LC	A65DC-2158	A50B-4001
1966	A50	A50R-101	A50C-101
	A50 Wasp	A50W-101	A50C-101
	A65 T'bolt	A65T-101	A50C-101
	A65 Lightning	A65L-101	A50C-101
	A65 Hornet	A65H-101	A50C-101
	A65 Spitfirelll	A65S-101	A50C-101

1967-on – engine and frame used the same number

Year	Model	Engine/Frame
1967	A50	A50RA-101
	A50 Wasp	A50WA-101
	A65 T'bolt	A65TA-101
	A65 Lightning	A65LA-101
	A65 Hornet	A65HA-101
	A65 Spitfirelll	A65SA-101
1968	A50	A50RB-101
	A50 Wasp	A50WB-101
	A65 T'bolt	A65TB-101
	A65 Lightning	A65LB-101
	A65 Hornet	A65HB-101
	A65 Spitfire	IVA65SB-101
1969	A50	A50RC-101
	A65 T'bolt	A65TC-101
	A65 Lightning	A65LC-101
	A65 Firebird	A65FC-101

During 1969, a new system used the first letter to denote month, the second for year, as follows:

	Month	Model	Year
A	January	C	1969
B	February	D	1970
C	March	E	1971
D	April	G	1972
E	May		
G	June		
H	July		
J	August		
K	September		
N	October		
P	November		
X	December		

1970 model codes: A50R, A65T, A65L, A65F
1971 model codes: A65T, A65L, A65FS, frame XE00101 on

1972 model codes: A65T, A65L, A70L, frame XG00101 on

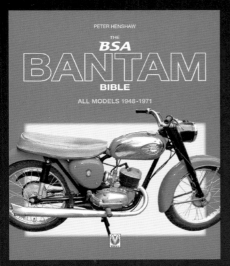

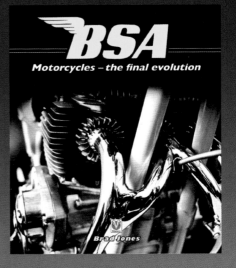

The Essential Buyer's Guide

VOLKSWAGEN **BUS**	Triumph **TR6**	MG **MGB MGB GT**	JAGUAR **E-type** V12 5.3 litre	CITROËN **2CV**	PORSCHE **928**	MORRIS **MINOR & 1000**
978-1-845840-22-8	978-1-845840-26-6	978-1-845840-29-7	978-1-845840-77-8	978-1-845840-99-0	978-1-904788-70-6	978-1-845841-01-0
JAGUAR/DAIMLER **XJ6, XJ12 & Sovereign**	MERCEDES-BENZ PAGODA **230, 250 & 280SL**	BMW **GS**	BSA **500 & 650 Twins**	CITROËN **DS & ID**	ROLLS-ROYCE **SILVER SHADOW** BENTLEY **T-SERIES**	FIAT **500 & 600**
978-1-845841-19-5	978-1-845841-13-3	978-1-845841-35-5	978-1-845841-36-2	978-1-845841-38-6	978-1-845841-46-1	978-1-845841-47-8
SUBARU **IMPREZA**	BSA **Bantam**	VOLKSWAGEN **GOLF GTI**	JAGUAR/DAIMLER **XJ40**	Jaguar/Daimler **XJ**	**MINI**	FORD **CAPRI**
978-1-845841-63-8	978-1-845841-65-2	978-1-845841-88-1	978-1-845841-92-8	978-1-845842-00-0	978-1-845842-04-8	978-1-845842-05-5
Triumph **STAG**	Norton **Commando**	Peugeot **205 GTI**	HONDA **SOHC FOURS**	TRIUMPH **TRIPLES & FOURS**	TRIUMPH **BONNEVILLE**	HARLEY-DAVIDSON **Big Twins**
978-1-845842-70-3	978-1-845842-81-9	978-1-845842-83-3	978-1-845842-84-0	978-1-845842-87-1	978-1-84584-134-8	978-1-845843-03-8
HONDA **CBR600 HURRICANE**	TRIUMPH **TR7 & TR8**	**CORVETTE** C2 Sting Ray	Porsche **911SC**	Vespa **SCOOTERS**	Porsche **911 (964)**	Porsche **911 (996)**
978-1-845843-09-0	978-1-845843-16-8	978-1-845843-29-8	978-1-845843-30-4	978-1-845843-34-2	978-1-845843-38-0	978-1-845843-39-7
JAGUAR **XJ-S**	MAZDA **MX-5 MIATA**	HONDA **CBR FireBlade**	Porsche **911 (993)**	LAND ROVER **SERIES I, II & IIA**	DUCATI **Bevel Twins**	PORSCHE **924**
978-1-845841-61-4	978-1-845842-31-4	978-1-845843-07-6	978-1-845843-40-3	978-1-845843-48-9	978-1-845843-63-2	978-1-845844-09-7

Index